When the World
BREAKS OPEN

WHEN THE
WORLD
Breaks Open

SEEMA REZA

RED HEN PRESS | PASADENA, CA

Book design and layout by Selena Trager

Library of Congress Cataloging-in-Publication Data
Names: Reza, Seema, author.
Title: When the world breaks open / Seema Reza.
Description: Pasadena : Red Hen Press, [2016]
Identifiers: LCCN 2015036152 | ISBN 9781597097444 (paperback)
Subjects: LCSH: Reza, Seema. | Authors, American—21st century—Biography. | Writing centers—Case studies. | BISAC: BIOGRAPHY & AUTOBIOGRAPHY / Personal Memoirs.
Classification: LCC PS3618.E986 Z46 2016 | DDC 811/.6—dc23
LC record available at http://lccn.loc.gov/2015036152

The Los Angeles County Arts Commission, the National Endowment for the Arts, the Pasadena Arts & Culture Commission and the City of Pasadena Cultural Affairs Division, Sony Pictures Entertainment, the Los Angeles Department of Cultural Affairs, the Dwight Stuart Youth Fund, and the Ahmanson Foundation partially support Red Hen Press.

First Edition
Published by Red Hen Press
www.redhen.org

Acknowledgments

Many thanks to the editors of the following print and online journals where portions of this manuscript, sometimes in slightly different versions, first appeared: *The Beltway Quarterly*, *Duende*, *Full Grown People*, *HerKind*, *Hermeneutic Chaos*, *The Manifestation*, *Pithead Chapel*, *Referential Magazine* and *Survive and Thrive: A Journal for Medical Humanities as Narrative and Medicine*.

Contents

I can't be a failure. I'm not done yet.

—*Ashley Russell*

Introduction

The title of this book is a fragment of a question my then five-year-old son asked in 2011, when we were reeling. From the sorrow seeping through our slowly dissolving nuclear family—his father and I had decided to separate, but continued to live together for sixteen months, sharing a house while we tried to discover which parts of ourselves could be salvaged from the wreckage. From the deaths, in close succession, of three beloved family members. From the emotional weight of the job I took doing arts programming at a military facility and the pressure of trying to maintain its funding.

At the time, "when" seemed to point to this particular era in our family's history, and the "breaking open" seemed linked to hardship. But I have since discovered that the world "opening" is an ongoing process of clarification, a stepping towards becoming myself. And there is no singular, chronologically-connected when. I have been wading into the murkiness of memory and extracting what I need to survive to make sense of what I am living. Just as often, new experiences have clarified the past. Most of the stories in this work take place between 2005 and 2012 but the world has been breaking open, in its beauty and grime, for a great deal longer than that, and continues to, even as I write this. What follows is a series of interconnected passageways I am still traveling.

Spark

There was a time
when your body and mine
could not control the spark
which turned to flame
and consumed us both.

Stasis

Le Chatelier's Principle: If a chemical system at equilibrium experiences a change in concentration, temperature, volume, or partial pressure, then the equilibrium shifts to counteract the imposed change and a new equilibrium is established.

This is optimism: seeing everything, *everything* wrong. Seeing it all entirely. And then, very carefully, choosing *not* to see it anymore. Choosing instead to find beauty, to let the worst things fade from focus, to shift to accommodate the unavoidable disappointments and changes in order to find balance. It is the way of the natural world. Necessary. Dangerous.

Such optimism is essential to existence in a place as poverty stricken and precariously positioned as Dhaka, Bangladesh. In 1971, east Pakistan divorced west Pakistan in a bloody civil war. East Pakistan became Bangladesh. The majority of the country's economic activity was agricultural then—fishing and farming—businesses and lives were tied to the tempers of the rivers crisscrossing the land on their paths to the Bay of Bengal. The people have tired of this relationship, so they migrate, 400,000 each year, to Dhaka city. Dhaka's population density is double that of New York City—more than 100,000 people occupy every square mile. People live in commercial high-rises and in dingy, one-room apartments above the markets, in gaudily appointed mansions and in small, family-owned buildings three or four stories high. As the concentration of people in the city grows, so does the city's volume: the fragile tin and bamboo shacks of slums mushroom and expand the borders of the city. Hopeful migrants work in garment factories and as household help in private homes; they pull bicycle rickshaws and beg in the muddy streets.

During the pre-monsoon, from March to August, the heat is dense and vicious, a physical force. The clouds bear down like a blanket still in place after the fever has broken and the city squirms and looks skyward. Children on the street, old men at roadside tobacco shops and women at tea parties anticipate the rain in every conversation. The monsoon invites the rivers, menacing and necessary as dictators, to encroach on the land, which is on average a mere six to eight meters above sea level. It will turn the city back into a swamp, and thousands of people will die of water-borne illness, pneumonia, or will simply drown. Slum-dwelling families fish up their floating belongings and wait on drier land. Bangladeshi folk songs praise the beauty of the rain and rivers. The monsoon is a monster, but it is also their savior. For in the height of the monsoon, when curtains of rain are parted daily by an hour or two of intense sunshine, rice crops grow at rates of five or six inches a day, remaining just ahead of the furious, rising water.

I met my husband, Karim, here in Dhaka. He was twenty and I was seventeen. We fell deep into a desperate, salty sort of love. I loved the way he looked at me and the way heads turned for us as a couple. I loved his dimples and his grace, his cool air in dark designer sunglasses. The Dhaka we inhabited was a series of rooftop parties and bottles of vodka bought on the black market for a middle-class man's monthly wages. We lifted the hems of our pants and stepped over the muck on our way into posh restaurants. When he punched the windshield of his car in anger, I was scared. But through an optimist's eye his jealousy proved his devotion; his forgiveness was divine. I saw an instant bridge to the future with him, free of our families, free of religion, independent, adult. We were married within a year and had our first child soon after, our second six years later.

Since then, I have been back to Dhaka with one son or both, with and without Karim. But now, for the first time in twelve years, at twenty-nine years old, I make the eight thousand mile journey entirely in my own company. Karim and the kids remain at our home in Maryland. There is no shoulder to rest my head upon, no children to care for. This visit to my family, a family in which I am a child rather than a mother, is intended to give me a break from cooking, cleaning, kids, and a respite from the tedium of my suburban life. The time apart will renew my marriage.

In a pale blue journal with handmade paper pages, I have written and illustrated a book for the children to read in my absence. The book begins: *When I am flying high over the ocean, you will be warm in your beds. Let's meet in our dreams and have mushroom soup up in the clouds.* After ten or eleven pages of meticulous writing, chronicling how we will stay connected in dreams in spite of distance and differing time zones, I run out of time and have to improvise. I put captions on pages and ask them to illustrate, tuck a Starbucks gift card between the blank pages in the back.

The night before my flight, as I haphazardly finish the book, I feel an uncontrolled sense of failure—of unpreparedness and guilt. My suitcase lays open, gifts for aunts and cousins still in shopping bags wait to be packed. Karim offers to help. He asks whether the shoes must be packed beside their mates, if tags should be removed from gifts, if I am sure my mother really needs this or that. Irritated, I snap at him once, then twice, and before I know it, it has spun out of control; he has snapped back and we are up all night. I am pulled into his spiral as he dives into one argument after the other: grievances a decade old follow new accusations of wasteful spending and concerns over my immodest wardrobe choices.

At the airport, I hold the children and weep. I smell their heads as if they are newborns. Karim spent the day sleeping while I ran all my last minute errands with the boys in tow. He woke two hours before I had to leave to catch my 9 p.m. flight. He checks my passport and tickets repeatedly. He moves my laptop from one compartment of my carry-on to another, fusses with the zipper on my suitcase—repenting through care for minutiae. When it is time for me to head toward the plane, I dodge his kiss and glide away down the escalator. By the time my plane touches down in London, I am ready to let go of my anger, to steady myself. I send him a text message from Heathrow to tell him I've landed and I remind myself of how lucky I am to have him.

The patchwork of green seen from the sky as the plane descends in Dhaka invites hope—perhaps it's not as bad as I remembered, perhaps in the three years since my last visit, sweeping changes have been made. The view soon gives way to a swarming cityscape dotted with coconut trees and once white buildings discolored by pollution and humidity-borne mold.

My luggage is slow to arrive and my parents, aunt and cousins have been waiting behind the metal gate outside the arrivals door for more than an hour. Finally one of my cousins pays a security guard five hundred taka to let him in to see what's keeping me. By then I am already rolling my parrot-green suitcase toward the door. There are no refunds on bribes.

My cousins make a big show of putting a garland of orange mums around my neck when I finally come out. They congratulate me on having traveled from America and ask me loudly if I need to use the bathroom. People stare, and our scene becomes louder. I assert that I am very busy and in America we all wear diapers to promote productivity. We laugh harder. The three of them were born and brought up in Dhaka but have spent the better part of the past ten years studying and working in New England, Canada and Singapore. We appreciate the instant audience afforded by a society in which it is not considered impolite to stare.

Homeostasis is the ability of the body or a cell to seek and maintain a condition of equilibrium or stability within its internal environment when dealing with external changes.

All horrors can be absorbed. Even the shock of poverty wears off. Before this happens, every sight feels like a slug to the chest. It takes more than an hour to travel three miles by automobile in the city at some times of day, and through the windows of the car I watch children carrying babies on their hips. Thirty-six percent of the population in Dhaka is under twelve. Kids tap on my window and beg and wave sheets of cheap stickers that I buy. I watch a child of two or three squat and have a bowel movement on the sidewalk. His mother picks up a green foil potato chip bag from the gutter and wipes him with it and then picks up the feces. Every day, I cry.

At a point in each trip, my heart begins to encase itself in armor: the working children who serve tea and cold drinks in households I visit socially, the mothers begging for rice to feed their babies, the haggard looking men and women breaking bricks by hand in the hot sun become nearly invisible. I realize the magnitude of the problem, recognize my own limitations and then give up and go about my own business. I talk on the phone or read a novel in traffic. I dip an edge of my cotton scarf in perfume and breathe through it when we pass through an especially malodorous part of the city. I adapt.

Soon, I begin to pick out beauty, find reasons to smile. The flowers, sticky fragrant, arranged in baskets to fan like peacock displays in neighborhood shops on nearly every main street. I admire the painted designs on the backs of bicycle rickshaws, the strings of lights spilling over the sides of wedding halls, the colorful bolts of checkered woven and floral printed fabrics stacked in the markets. I make offerings of paper boxes of milk and foil packages of biscuits to children in the street to ease my conscience, and feel good about what I've done. This skin of optimism is thin, permeable. I go shopping with my mother and am suddenly faced with a child of nine or ten, the same age as my older son, pulling antiques from a case and presenting them to me. I smile and ask whether he goes to school. His smile fades, and I realize I have embarrassed him. My chest constricts.

My mother has the smiling, dimpled, childlike confidence and self-assurance that come from being loved and of believing in her beauty. Her only nod to vanity is black hair-dye—and even that she often forgets to do. She has left us behind, reversing her forty-year migration to the United States to retire and return to the city of her childhood. She has traded beloved indulgent weekends with her grand-children and daily conversations with her daughters for an apartment across the hall from her octogenarian mother and stepfather, who suffers from dementia. In Dhaka, she is "grandmother" to a group of the city's poorest children. They attend a need-based school; only the least fortunate are accepted. They are mostly fatherless children whose mothers work as washerwomen and prostitutes. In addition to a traditional education, they receive lessons in hygiene. Each child bathes in the morning upon arrival at school. Signs posted around the open courtyard of the one-story building read Don't spit and Wear shoes in Bengali and English. With their uniforms they receive a bag of rice, a bag of sugar, and a can of cooking oil for their families each month. My mother adds the fun. She takes them on trips to amusement parks and treats the whole school to ice cream and coke. She kisses and hugs them and remembers their names as well as she can.

She says she loves it here in Dhaka. She loves that she is finally home. In her time in America, she sought out hard to find tropical flavors: squash greens, dried mango, fiery little green chilies. She ate rice every day. Here in Dhaka, she bakes cupcakes and signs up for an Italian cooking class at the American Embassy Club. She asks me to bring cake mixes and tubs of icing in my suitcase. Now Duncan Hines tastes like home.

She asks about Karim and the children daily. I tell her the highlights: Karim's promotion, Sam's wisdom, Zaki's clever mischief. She can sense something is not right, and she is nearly always by my side. She sleeps with an arm over me in the giant bed she brought in a shipping container from America, and wakes me with a cup of tea. She reminds me to call Karim, to email him, wonders how he'll feel about this or that. I try to respond evenly. But when I come out of the bedroom after a harrowing long-distance telephone conversation with Karim, she sees my face and I tell her, *I don't think I can do this. He is so unhappy.*

I have spent my time in Dhaka basking in her confidence and regaining my own. I have stopped taking the anti-depressant I begged the psychiatrist for in an effort to save my marriage. I have laughed and been easy to be around. I have avoided my father, who loves Karim so much that I can't trust him. For a brief moment, my mother forgets the professional photograph hung on her wall of Karim and me, posed in an embrace, left hands clasped, the wedding bands we nearly forgot to wear reflecting the studio lights. She forgets, and she says, *No, no. You can't live like this. You can't go on this way.*

To her, divorce is the worst thing that can happen to anyone. Her own experience as a child of divorce, over half a century ago, still haunts her. It is the reason she immediately takes back her words. *Try counseling*, she says. *Try something.*

Newton's First Law of Motion: Every body remains in a state of rest or uniform motion unless acted upon by an external unbalanced force.

There are times when radical change just cannot be avoided. For Bangladesh, that time came in 1970, when unrest over the lack of Bangla representation in the Pakistani government was compounded with fury over the lag in the government response time to the ferocious Bhola Cyclone, which hit in November of that year. Over half a million people were killed, crops were destroyed, villages leveled. Bangladesh went into its fight for liberation wounded. She paid, with self-destruction and the virtue of her daughters and the lives of her sons. She stood shakily triumphant, blinking in the light—she had never maintained her own economy or governed herself. But she had reclaimed her identity and had hope for her future.

My grandmother is in love. She is no optimist. To her, nearly everyone is an asshole—just wait and they'll prove it. But with her husband, she is sweet and trusting. More so since his dementia has begun to steadily march across their life. He reaches for her hand and she allows him to take it, embarrassed by the show of affection, but pleased to be one of the few he truly remembers. She has withdrawn. She was never a loud person—her voice trembles and squeaks when pushed to high volume and even her laughter is a nearly silent heaving. She covers her face with the loose end of her sari and shakes, emitting only the high-pitched intake of her breath, as though she might be sobbing—though she would never show sorrow so plainly. When the family gathers and conversation and laughter reach a crescendo of absurdity, each of us talking over the others, she stands up and shuffles away, the black border of her white sari hovering two inches above the ground.

I bring her *TED Talks* to watch. She was a psychology professor at Dhaka University, and I've downloaded the lectures of Philip Zimbardo, Michael Sherner, and Dan Gilbert. They speak on the human capacity for evil, strange beliefs, and happiness. Morning after morning she half-watches, folding and unfolding her hands, adjusting the large glasses that magnify her already large eyes, crossing and uncrossing her ankles.

Hmm. Very interesting, she says.

In fact, nothing seems to interest her. We make conversation over tea. She is careful to ask after Karim and the children; I remember to ask after her knees and heart. But the real conversation, when we arrive at it, is both less material and more concrete. She asks me why I do not believe in God and what I do believe. I tell her I'm okay without knowing, that I can live without heaven if it means I can discard hell. She is religious; she prays regularly, a collection of prayer beads hangs on a hook on her bedroom wall. My step-grandfather is an atheist, but she can no longer ask these questions of him.

As the man my grandmother loves slowly recedes, she has more time to reflect on the man she didn't love. My biological grandfather was a taboo topic when I was a child, broached only when my mother and her two sisters, one older and one younger, thought all the kids were asleep. In the darkened room we shared on our summer vacations in Dhaka, out of the earshot of my grandmother, they compared memories and updates acquired through the Dhaka grapevine. In the daylight, they pretended to feel no loss, pretended so well, in fact, that many of my cousins can recall the electric shock of the exact moment they found out that our grandfather was not a biological relation. Even today, in spite of its twelve million people, the Dhaka of the English-speaking upper class is a relatively small town. In the early 1960s, it was smaller, more like an extended family. My grandparents' divorce and my grandmother's subsequent remarriage was a big deal. To quash any femme fatale accusations, my grandmother dressed in widow's white after her divorce. The austerity of her dress and the smooth neatness of her bun are juxtaposed by her partiality to things that sparkle: she wears a diamond ring on every finger, a large round-cut stone perches on her nose, clusters of diamonds drag her earlobes down.

My grandmother does not forgive. People who show her disloyalty are removed from her life. Upon their divorce, she systematically removed her children's father from every aspect of their lives and her own. At the beginning, she allowed their daughters to spend occasional afternoons with him, but when they returned home, she berated them for accepting the gifts he gave them. She told them that his mistress would be their stepmother and would beat them and torture them. Soon my mother and her sisters, terrified, refused to visit him. When he remarried, my grandmother returned the jewelry she had received at their wedding by having her cousin deliver it at his wedding reception on a silver tray and stopped speaking of him. Now my grandmother talks about her ex-husband openly and bitterly. She asks, *How many people can say they have been married to a true pervert? I can!* And we shake with laughter.

In Bangladeshi culture, family ties and lineage are the foundation of one's identity. While the caste system has no official place in an Islamic society, the successes of ancestors increase social standing and make young men and women more marriageable. Regardless of class, people meeting for the first time will ask one another, *Where is your home?* The question does not refer to one's current address—that question, *Where do you stay*—is far less telling. Your *home* is the village that your paternal ancestry can be traced to. The divorce was an amputation for my mother and aunts.

When my three weeks in Dhaka are up, I feel renewed. For a few weeks, I am unflappable, superwoman. I cook the children's favorite foods and reorganize the closets. I apply for jobs, plan a future for myself, have nights out with friends. I tell the psychiatrist to forget the pills. I tell Karim, *It's not me. I'm happy when you're not around.*

But the immobility returns, a force of its own. *He's not so bad*, I tell myself. *He never breaks a bone or blacks an eye.* I remind myself that I am difficult to live with, that it's my fault as much as his. *Nobody's perfect.*

We struggle along, presenting our offbeat perfection to the outside world as we always have. We play our parts: I am silly, child-like, spoiled. He is serious, accomplished, caring. We are beautiful together. We wear hip clothes to Sam's basketball games in a middle school gymnasium and sit with Zaki between us and cheer. We take the kids to nice restaurants and collect praise about their behavior from the wait-staff and other patrons. Months pass.

Then my friend accuses Karim of making advances toward her. When I confront him he denies it, says it was *she* who made the advances, and *he* who rebuffed them. I decide that the three of us should have this conversation in one place, together.

We meet in a park on a Sunday afternoon and they each tell their own side of the story, ladies first. When it is his turn, she interrupts his narrative, shouting, *Don't lie!*

He turns to her, fists balled; his features hard and sharp like a wooden mask. I know this face and quickly stand between them.

What are you going to do? She asks confidently. *Hit me?*

She is one of my closest friends. But she doesn't know. The key to equilibrium is absorption. Everything must be dissolved into the solution, stirred and warmed. If you say something aloud, it never goes away. And when Karim reaches his arms around me and pushes her by the neck, the solution becomes over-saturated. It is no longer liquid at all. It is another thing entirely, solid, concentrated. This is the point from which I cannot return, the point at which internal stability can no longer be maintained, and I am forced into motion.

Spineless

One night I dreamt my spine was separating from my body. My ribs moved lower and lower until I gave birth to my backbone. It lay on the bedspread with a bit of my pelvis attached, curved like a comma, it looked like the skeleton of a fish. I wanted to hold it, but was afraid it might break. It wasn't painful; it was almost freeing to allow my flesh to wobble uninterrupted. But I made an appointment with my doctor.

I told Karim, *You have to take me to the doctor. I have to have this checked out.*

You should *have it checked out. Definitely. I'll watch the kids, you take my car.* He said. His fingers never stopped their rapid clicking of the keys on his laptop.

You won't drive me?

Oh, I can't right now. Besides, we have the kids. We can't take them to a doctor's office. They might get sick.

I cradled my backbone in my arms, and went to the car. I put the seatbelt on it in the passenger's seat and got into the driver's seat where I could keep an eye on it.

I woke on my back, arms by my side, afraid to move.

Jellyfish

It was a particularly awful summer. A particularly *poor* summer, and though there were plenty of free things to do in the city, the crushing gloom of debt hung over Karim and me and we fought: about money, about time, about who was at fault for the myriad messes our life seemed to be dissolving into. I had every intention of giving in, making compromises, keeping the peace. But inevitably there was some comment or tone I could not ignore, some compromise I couldn't bear to make and all the eggshells I'd been trying not to crack turned to dust at once.

In an effort to change direction, we agreed to spend one Saturday doing something with the children. There was rain in the forecast. Karim got up late. The house was a mess. But I was determined. The Chesapeake Bay was an hour's drive from our house, and though I hadn't been since my own childhood, the memory was clear: slimy lengths of seaweed, rough, pebbled sand, brackish water. We packed the children into the car and sped northeast along the highway. In the backseat, our eight-year-old son Sam wore his swimsuit; goggles poised on top of his head as though he might leap from the car at any moment. Zaki, six years younger, slept open-mouthed in his car seat.

As we forewent the exit toward my parents' house in silence, I imagined living with them still, watching network television in the always-dim house while my mother cooked for the week and placed her loud rounds of cross-country phone calls—cousin in Chicago, aunt in Texas, friend in Seattle. Would I make excuses to leave the house and wander the shopping mall smelling of fried onions? I put my hand on Karim's leg. He brought his right hand down from the steering wheel and placed it lightly on mine. I flipped my hand over and gave his a squeeze. He did not squeeze back.

The parking lot at the beach was starting to clear. Everyone else had started the day early, like good people, real grownups with kids, should. We were arriving late, we forgot a picnic and we were barely getting along. We parked and unpacked the car, taking Zaki out last; he had woken sweaty and bewildered. We changed him to a swim diaper and gave him an empty blue plastic bucket to carry and Karim held his hand while I carried the towels and gracelessly tried to keep up with Sam's light steps toward the water; my feet sinking into the sand. Sam continued toward the water when I stopped to spread the blanket, securing it from the wind at the corners with the weight of the towels. Zaki and Karim made slow progress, pausing often to admire seagulls and rocks. When they stopped next to me I fastened Zaki's wide-brimmed cotton sun hat beneath his chin, kissing his firm fleshy cheek, still hot and red from sleep. Karim cocked his head to the side.

Don't you think we're a little close to those people over there?

I watched Karim walk Zaki to the water, timing each of his long steps to equal three of Zaki's shuffling toddler steps. When he was close enough, he took Sam's hand and led both children carefully into the water. When the water began to get deep, Karim lifted Zaki, still clutching the bucket with one fist, onto his hip and he and Sam continued to step deeper in, hesitantly. I walked behind them to the water's edge.

Before long, Sam pointed in the green-brown water to what looked like a wad of toilet paper floating a few feet away. A jellyfish. When we felt bold and approached it, tried to capture it in Zaki's blue bucket, the currents of the bay pulled it out of reach. When we stood still, unsure of how to proceed, it came nearer, frightening us, and we shied away.

Taste

The first week of my cycle I crave sour: dark, round globs of tamarind concentrate nested in the depressions of teaspoons, blackening my tongue, sticking my teeth. I lick wedges of lemon after they've been squeezed and pucker my lips, closing my mouth tight against what I should have said.

The second week of my cycle I need cold: frozen peas crunch feebly before surrendering between my teeth. Ice water soothes my sternum, quiets my belly, calms my nerves. I curl pats of sorbet in my tongue and when I unfurl it, all that rolls off is calculated, rational, detached.

The third week of my cycle I want only sugar: honey glistening on warm slices of cake, frothy peaks of whipped cream expelled from the can. Velvet slabs of cheesecake stay thick in my mouth, cling to my palate, wait patiently until I am through with them. The sweetness lingers in the corners of my lips, I catch it on the tip of my tongue and the words I form are gentle, kind, ingratiating.

The fourth week of my cycle I seek out fire: scalding tea the brown of my skin, wasabi peas that crunch and burn, oily pickled mangoes and carrots flecked with pepper seeds. The spiced bag of hot mix includes raisins to temper the heat and I discard them, allowing my breath to turn to smoke. When my mouth opens, poison rushes out.

And then I crave flesh: I trace the smooth, uneven scar on your shoulder with my tongue, take your chin—bristled, soft and hard—into my mouth. I bite your hands, scrape my teeth along the innocence of your earlobes. I lick the sorrowful sourness from your lips, pull your sweetness inside me, inhale your fury.

Head Wounds

He never hit me hard enough to break a bone. I didn't get black eyes or bruised cheeks. There was a burn on my arm from the oven rack and my sister asked pointedly, "Did he burn you with a cigarette?" And I said, "No, of course not." And really, he didn't. Wouldn't. I wonder if it was calculated—if he held back to keep himself safe. Or if maybe he really didn't want to hurt me that badly. One night he pushed me off the bed and my head hit the nightstand and I left a misshapen maroon pool on the carpet. When I opened my eyes in the morning, the stain had turned black. I looked closer and the spot was covered with ants. I hadn't known there were ants in the bedroom.

He brought me tea in bed and cleaned the blood up with OxiClean and a towel while I watched. *I'm sorry, head wounds bleed a lot. I'm sorry, but it's true*, he told me.

Sanity

We were strained in a way that made my teeth hurt. I reached out in little unreciprocated gestures—favorite dinners, funny stories. I came home one night and his posture flipped a switch in me and set my insides on fire. When I opened my mouth, I reduced him to ash. It was more than I'd meant to say, but I couldn't stop. And when I saw how wild I was being—rage of that caliber is an out of body experience—I surrendered to it completely. I lay my arms down, clenched my fists and let it pour forth. When I was done, he began. His insults weren't eloquent, but he slammed pots and kicked cabinets and jabbed me in the ribs and collarbone with his finger for emphasis. I was relieved that he was crazy too and I thought it would be over, that enduring his crazy would serve as penance for my own.

Late that night I went to deliver an apology wrapped in forgiveness, to smooth things over. He was sitting in the corner of the couch watching television with his brows furrowed, the remote poised in his right hand. He lifted his eyes briefly when I entered the room. I delivered my speech, familiarly specked with ardent defenses and wan confessions and he said, "I think I want a divorce."

Eventually, after much cajoling and rephrasing of questions on my part, he admitted that he didn't *want* a divorce. He wanted sanity.

"Sanity, sure. I can do that," I said. He finally accepted my apology—refusing my offer of forgiveness—and returned my kiss with a disdainful peck. I was trembling and giddy, like someone who has narrowly escaped a falling object. I resolved to do sanity right this time. We pulled a crisp sheet over our anger and tucked the edges in. For a time we were again polite paper dolls.

Long Weekend

We are in the car. I began working full-time a few weeks ago, and my entire second paycheck will be spent on this Memorial Day vacation. Occasionally, the female voice of the GPS interrupts the radio to remind us to proceed on the current highway. We are going to spend the weekend in the hills of western Maryland. The resort website boasts a swimming pool and shooting clays, horseback riding and s'mores by the fire, golf lessons and hiking trails. That Karim has a conference nearby is a happy coincidence. But this resort—discovered during an Internet search for Maryland resorts—was our destination regardless. We are mother and sons, off to do things we haven't done before. I have begun to change.

It is raining and dark by the time we get going. The roads are slick, but traffic moves at a steady pace. Brake lights flash. The car to our left has to swerve into the median to avoid hitting the car in front of it. I see the sparks from the scraping of metal against concrete and speed up—I don't want to be caught behind an accident. In the rearview mirror I watch the car hurtle sideways across four lanes of the highway, crossing over the space we just sped out of.

SATURDAY MORNING.

We wake in the hotel room, the boys in one bed and Karim and I in the other. He is rushing off to his workshop and we are making an itinerary for ourselves. Sam is signed up for a golf lesson; aside from that, it is up to us. We decide we will wear bathing suits all day.

SATURDAY EVENING.

We have dinner in the hotel restaurant. There is a lacrosse game on the television directly across from us, and I am astonished by the brutality of the game. I signed Sam up for a week of lacrosse camp in the coming summer, thinking that he might enjoy it, but now I realize I had no idea what lacrosse was. I couldn't imagine that a game played with nets on sticks could be so barbaric, and now Sam and I are eating dinner with our mouths wide open, terrified of what's ahead.

SUNDAY AFTERNOON.

The boys and I meet Karim for lunch a few miles from the hotel after his last conference session ends. I can tell that Karim's mood has shifted. The boys and I spent the morning in the sunshine, swimming in the lake and taking photographs of birds. I believe that the only reason he could possibly be in a bad mood is because I've done something. *Is this a form of narcissism?* I cannot understand how he can be upset when we have been apart all day. The darkness of the cool, wood-paneled restaurant is disorienting, and I feel dizzy, very nearly drunk. When we return to the hotel, I suggest that Karim get a massage. Instead we go to the driving range. Afterward, as we leave the hotel to get ice cream, Zaki bumps into the sliding glass door. He turns to Karim, who is holding his hand, and begins to cry. *That was your fault, Baba! You made me do it.*

I did not! Karim replies through gritted teeth. *That was your own fault.*

Zaki's lip begins to tremble and I know this will only get worse. I let go of Sam's hand and step between Karim and Zaki.

Why don't you go to the car, we'll catch up. Karim and Sam walk toward the car and Zaki and I discuss whether birds can read street signs (he says they can read the yellow ones). When we get to the car, I ask Karim if maybe he'd like me to take the boys for ice cream while he takes a nap.

Why? I'm fine. He smiles in a way that doesn't crinkle the edges of his eyes.

At the restaurant, I am so tense I can't bear to have ice cream. Instead I order a cup of soup.

Sunday Evening.

We are walking down the hall towards the hotel room. Karim and I are holding hands. We tell the children not to run. They run. They jostle; Sam pushes Zaki. Karim lets go of my hand and takes off his shoes as he runs toward them. I smile. He is running to beat them both in the race, to resolve the issue altogether. I admire his parenting. He slows as he reaches them, widely swings the brown flip-flop in his right hand to swat Sam's bottom. He drags him into the room. The world shifts.

Zaki and I enter the room. Sam is laying on the bed nearest the door on his right side, hands up, shoulders hunched. Karim is standing over him, barefoot, brandishing his shoe.

I get in front of Karim, put my hands on my hips. *You are acting fucking crazy.*

I've got another shoe for you. Saliva flies from his mouth.

Get out. Get out of my hotel room. Get out. This is my vacation. Get out. I have never felt so sure of anything.

He leaves, and I send him a text message. *You need to get help for your anger or our marriage is over.* I tell Sam, *I don't know if I can keep doing this.*

The children and I cry ourselves to sleep.

Counseling

We go to see a counselor. Karim will not accept that he should see someone for his anger, but agrees to couples' therapy. I will take what I can get. Based on the bio on the office's website, it appears that the primary focus of this therapist's career has been on issues of gender identity and homosexuality. But she is available on the day we need, and I don't want Karim's compliance to dissipate. Lainey has short hair, thick wire-rimmed glasses, black socks and orthopedic shoes.

Karim tells the story of the hotel room. In his retelling, Sam's push sent Zaki flying headfirst into the wall. *He could have seriously hurt him. It was unacceptable.*

I see, Lainey says. *So you wanted to make a strong statement.*

Yes. And then Seema challenged my authority in front of the kids. I got mad. I shouldn't have said that to her.

It seems so simple, so reasonable explained this way. I wonder if I've been overreacting all along. Maybe we're not so badly off. Maybe we just have a few little issues.

She asks Karim, *Why do you want to stay married?*

Because of the kids. And she can't afford to be on her own.

She turns to me. *Seema, what do you think about that?*

My teeth are white, my hair is thick. I *know* this man, know that he loves me. I laugh. *That's bullshit. I'm an excellent cook and the sex is fantastic.*

For the rest of the summer and into the fall, we see Lainey nearly every Monday evening. Lainey prods us to say kind things about one another, and encourages us to implement date nights.

In October, after he pushed my friend and changed my perspective, shook me from my slumbering pretense, we go back to see Lainey. I have decided that I have outgrown the fight. Now, he begs me to visit the therapist one last time. I agree, taking along a ball of wool and knitting needles. We sit in the now familiar office, meeting at our regular time, but days are shorter and the room is darker than usual. He begins to talk and I begin to knit. He catalogues my crimes: making him jealous at seventeen, rekindling a friendship with an old boyfriend at twenty, disliking his mother from the start, dancing with another man at a nightclub one night. He tells it chronologically, has clearly been rehearsing this narrative—collecting the evidence.

Several times anger rises up from my core, forces my mouth to fall open, but I knit more furiously, shut my mouth. I am determined to give him this opportunity. After thirty minutes, Lainey interrupts him. The clock is ticking, he needs to wrap up. He moves to my most recent crimes: not believing him when he said he didn't make advances toward my friend, forcing him to have to push her because he felt backed into a corner, because he thought we were ganging up against him. Forty of our fifty minutes are up.

Lainey looks at me. *Seema?*

I look up from my knitting. I let it fall to my lap, push my glasses up. I take a deep breath. *I'm done.* For a moment I consider responding to the accusations he has made, defending myself, remind him that he has left out his responsibility in all of it. But the feeling evaporates with my exhale. *I don't want to do this anymore.*

Okay, she says. *Let's talk about divorce counseling.*

Afterward, Karim is livid. *How could she have given up on us like that? What kind of counselor is she? It's your fault. Why were we seeing a social worker anyway?* He goes to see a therapist on his own, and tells me that therapist said we shouldn't get divorced. *That* therapist thinks that Lainey was wrong to have told us what to do.

She didn't tell us what to do. I told her I was done.

You told her you were done after she told us to get divorce counseling.

The order of things is always uncertain with us. He remembers it one way, I remember it another.

Dragging

He has told me to leave countless times over the past eleven years. Pulled to the door, dragged by my ankle or arm, sometimes by my hair. With his free hand he wrenches open the door. I plead with him, clinging to the lip of the step or the banister or the leg of a table. He doesn't really want me to go; it's an exercise. If I try to leave of my own accord, he blocks my way and confiscates my keys. It is the struggle, the exertion of power. He can put me out when he wants and he can keep me here if he wishes because this is *his* house.

Later, I can never remember what I said or did beforehand; can't recall the exact moment the argument spun out of control. I must have delivered some venom with enunciated precision. Maybe I even landed the first blow; invited the adrenaline rush borne of conflict.

When our marriage is finally over, we both know there is no turning back. I have learned that I am no longer to blame for his flaws. He has learned that I have feelings for another man. He tells me I should leave, really this time. Get an apartment. He says that he can't sleep when I am under his roof.

I feel bad for him, and guilty for being done. I begin to make arrangements. I respond to ads for tiny apartments that I can barely afford, attempt to feel excited at the prospect of having my own space. I try not to think about the loss of mornings with my sons; about the shrunken time I will spend with them.

My car is in the shop and he is working from home. I ask him if I can take his car to teach art at our older son's school and then pick both children up. He holds the keys up a few feet away and says, *Why should I give you my car? You should have made your own arrangements.* He calls me a cunt and a whore and says he doesn't trust me with the children or the car. I ask again and again for the keys. Finally, I call the school and tell them I can't make it today. I pack my laptop, wallet, and water bottle into a backpack. I need to work on my paper. I head for the door.

Who's going to pick up the kids? He calls after me.

I turn the key in the lock.

Deserter, he shouts.

During my short walk to the coffee shop he calls me nineteen times. I answer twice and hear him try to talk me in circles, asking questions that have no right answer. The courthouse is a block further and I decide to go there instead. I sign in at the free legal clinic and wait for two hours. I feel embarrassed to take out my shiny laptop and work while sitting among the tired, confused looking people who populate the waiting area. But my time is limited, and my work needs to get done.

When my name is called, I follow a gray-haired attorney to a cubicle. I sit on the outside of the L shaped desk and he looks at my income statement. He tells me I make too much money to be here. *But you've waited and you seem like a nice person, so let's talk.*

I tell him that I need to move out, but I can't afford any place near our home, and certainly no place where the children will be comfortable.

Why do you need to move out?

Because he can't sleep, and I can't pay the mortgage by myself, I say.

There's no cure for assholes, the lawyer says. He smiles. His teeth are white and straight and his hair is thinning. He wears a thick silver-toned wedding band. *He can't sleep. Tough shit. Do not move out. You don't have to.* He sits back and tells me about my entitlement to alimony and child support. *You can be accommodating, sure. Avoid all conflict. It'll make things easy for him, and you'll get screwed.*

When I come home, Karim has picked the kids up and they are eating a snack. He can see that something has shifted. It makes him antsy.

We'll talk about it later, I tell him.

He presses me, but I refuse to say anything with the kids around. When they go to bed, we sit at the kitchen table and I tell him that I know I have options; that I will move out when I can afford to move to a place where the children are comfortable and safe.

His demeanor changes. He is crying now, says, *I have seen the error of my ways.* His word choice disgusts me. Fat tears fall onto my kitchen table and dampen my resolve. I pick up a dishtowel and wipe them away.

I meet his eyes, look at him hard. *Remember that girl you dragged around, who wanted to smooth things over, make things easy? I've got her by the hair now.*

Texts

Alisha Stoneman has been texting my husband. Well, technically my husband. Unofficially, he's my soon to be ex-husband. But we still live together. Her daughter is in our younger son's preschool class. I feel affronted. How dare she? She is no match for me. She is taller and skinnier but not prettier and absolutely not better dressed. She is married. For all she knows, Karim is married.

What do you care? He asks me, amused. *Our marriage is over. Remember?*

Yes, of course I remember, I tell him. *It's not about you. It's about me. If I decide in my head to give away my couch but then someone comes into my house and takes it, that's still stealing. Until I put the damn thing on the curb, she better keep her hands off of it.*

Forgiveness

I replay the last year of our marriage: the hotel hallway, his refusal to seek counseling, his stance against apology, his violence towards my friend. I wonder if I should have used different words, made him feel safer. Instead of turning to my friends, to another man, I wonder if I should have turned to him in those weeks when he said he was willing to do anything to keep me. And then I feel angry at my weakness for thinking these thoughts, for letting his words creep into my psyche, and the anger swings back to point at him. But in the stilling of this pendulum lies great risk.

Underneath the clanging racket of anger, in the quiet beyond the threshold of forgiveness, lies a love that makes no sense, that doesn't hold up under the light of reason. The same love I felt at seventeen and twenty-eight. A love that consumed me, consumes me still. How do I forget that love? I have experience in forgetting the bad times, the anger, the vicious words, the arguments and blame. But how can I forget the feeling of his rough cheek against my hand, of my fingertip traveling down the line of his smooth forehead along his nose? The smell of his neck. The hard jut of his collarbone, the round of his shoulders in my palms.

If I isolate the good, allow myself to remember the feeling of him coming home from work, of the lift in my heart from hearing his keys in the door, of seeing the door open and him standing there with his bag over his shoulder, sunglasses on his handsome head, the appearance of his dimples as the boys thudded down the stairs toward him, the kicking off of his shoes, his ascent from the foyer, the completeness of those moments, when we were four together under one roof, I am overcome by a grief from which I can barely surface.

Maybe I Don't Forgive
So Easily Either

*An unedited excerpt of email I sent to myself a year before I decided
to leave*

When the threat is gone, when the need for the tension
to dissipate has passed and you are yet again fooling me,
charming me into believing that the great dad and caring
husband are all I need to remember, I feel like you owe me.
Since I am not given an apology, I will take one. I punish
you by disrespecting you, by saying nasty things and deval-
uing the work you do. So the cause and effect isn't so linear.

Hitting me while I have a resting baby in my arms? Awful,
but not a first. There are so few firsts left for you in that
realm. He knew what you were doing, Sam knew what you
were doing. And yet you continued to punch me in my back
and ribs. To threaten to kill me. And yet you continue to
blame me for any damage done to your relationship with
your kids. They are learning to avoid you when the warning
signs are flashing. I hope they can teach me, or that I can
find the strength to head in another direction.

—Seema Reza
October 9, 2009

Flash

We are all good enough to get better.

Swallowing Sadness

I know the prompt I'm going to do, I've worked with most of these patients. I know the too small room, the cluster of rectangular tables pushed together in the center, an odd assortment of office junk at one end—filing cabinets, a desk in the front where the tech will sit to make sure no one kills me.

I have remembered to wear a diamond ring on the ring finger on my left hand and the three-inch stack of bangles that will announce my movements so I startle no one.

Once everyone sits down and we've made some small talk and handed out pens and composition books, I introduce myself for anyone new and deliver my opening statement. I tell them I am a writer, not a therapist. I tell them that whatever trauma brought them here will not be the last. I can't promise much, but I can promise you that. Life will keep hitting you. Writing is what I believe in most of all, writing has saved my life. Writing saves my life on a regular basis. I tell them this.

I pass around print out of Katie Regan's "When Your Mother is a Drug Addict," from *Pithead Chapel*. There are some murmurs, some jokes as the title is read. We go around the room and read it, one paragraph at a time.

This is a substance abuse program, and my initial intention was to use this prompt to ask people to look at them-

selves honestly, as the center from which pain ripples outward. But for most it's too soon. They have to look first at
themselves as the ones caught in the wake of other histories
of pain. I have done this prompt before, I know how powerful it will be. Today my own life is a mess. I am going out
of town later this week and feel the guilt of abandoning my
children. I would prefer not to metabolize all of this, but
I know where these folks are and I know they need to be
shaken up.

As they write I can feel the air in the room quiver. Their
faces hold looks of confusion, of disorientation, as if they
have suddenly found themselves here. But everyone is willing to share and we go around the room.

> *When your father says you are special*
> *When your father keeps a gun in the car*
> *When your parents are neglectful*
> *When your favorite uncle is an alcoholic*
> *When your grandpa is paranoid*
> *When your aunt is an angel, she takes your uncle's beatings like a*
> *champ*

The group is supposed to end at 2:20, at 2:45 the last story
is still going. The air in the room is charged, as if we are sitting in an electrical fog. I keep my tears invisible, smile at
each person, actively push love at each person as they read.
Inside, my heart cleaves, splits like wood. I feel myself sway.
I press my palms together, thank them for their courage,
their honesty, their trust. I wish I could enclose them, protect the children they were. I sit in these rooms swallowing
sadness, like a fish trying to drink the ocean.

Odyssey

We are taking turns reading *The Odyssey* aloud. It is an illustrated children's version, in which *the wine dark sea* churns ominously on most pages. I read while the children eat their dinner, they read while I sip tea. In a half-custody household, you work twice as hard to finish what you started.

I recognize noble, courageous, burdened Odysseus—at once aware of his powerlessness and narcissistic enough to suffer from guilt over that which is beyond his control.

Here is the whirling tide pool that threatens to suck him in and spit him out, battered and gasping. Threatens to crush his vessel and thrust him to the surface, clinging to splinters, exposed.

The Night

I am a woman halfway through life, children flung out from me like seeds, unfurling from familiar shapes. Still, occasionally they return to curl into the softness of my body, round hard skulls and knees pushing into my yielding abdomen, the hollow beneath my arm.

The walls have dissolved, the suit of secrets has fallen, and I am flung into the night myself. I am a woman whose hands are capable, who braces at promises, tries to grow cold to expectation and float blindly on a tumble of cold waves. I use imagined futures like oars until one by one I release them and they drift away behind me.

I have come to the place borne of fire and ruin, where the landscape shifts at the lightest touch like a pile of ash. They show me their scars, their sharp fright, their blood and suffering. My work is to stare into all their yellow eyes without blinking, to steady the table while they shake it.

Fear

I had my first nightmare when I was four. I had the chickenpox and dreamed that Raggedy Ann and Andy came over to play and knocked over the fishbowl. The most terrifying thing I had ever seen was the flopping of the goldfish as they were pulled from the water in the long-handled green net when the tank was cleaned.

I have a nightmare that someone is following me in a car as I'm walking on a bridge. I run, but can't get away. I know that I am dreaming, but when I open my eyes, all I can see is the inside of my eye mask and the darkness returns me to the bridge.

I discontinue the medication.

When I was seven, I watched *Child's Play* with my mother and sisters. In this movie, a doll goes on a killing spree. For years I had to put my dolls out of sight before I could sleep. It's possible that I never outgrew this fear at all, but outgrew playing with dolls.

Charlie visits with the soldier who replaced him in his unit after he was injured. The replacement soldier was himself injured within twelve hours, and Charlie goes to see him every day. I ask if he can leave the hospital. *He's allowed to leave, but he doesn't want to. They tell us we're safe now, but we've spent so much time being afraid we don't believe them.*

I have another nightmare. I am on post after a long day of work. Everywhere I go rapists lurk in the shadows. I outrun them. Finally, another woman offers me a ride, getting out of her car to flag me down. As I get in, someone grabs her. I don't get out to help. I drive away in her car to save myself. I know that I am not strong enough to save her. When I wake, I am frozen in bed, my heart pounding, my throat dry. I wonder how people live like this.

At the art table, patients discuss their nightmares. Not the particulars of them but the fact of them, the ways they cope with them. Therapy dogs trained for nightmare interruption and the many sleep meds they've tried. *When I went home for Christmas, my parents told me I scream in my sleep.* Another responds, *Yeah, my ex-boyfriend told me the same thing.* The effect of the medication they are taking is that you don't remember the nightmares. But how can the body not remember?

We are eating lunch in the hospital cafeteria. My dining companion is a Marine who works here. He has deployed four times and will be leaving again in a month, first to train new recruits in the desert in California and then to lead them into battle. He eats with his elbows on the table, broad shoulders hunched. He has a burst blood vessel in his left eye. It flashes as he surveys the room between bites. *You know that feeling you get, when you wake up to a noise in the middle of the night and you feel like there's someone in the house?* I nod. *That's what it's like down-range. The whole time.*

While We Sleep

Zaki drags his sleeping bag to the floor
next to my bed, shin guards fastened
around his lengthening legs, a stack of
skewers (he calls them *spears*)—beside
him, flashlight under his pillow. He has
placed a chair against the front door of our
apartment. He says he is running security.

> *Across the world, a boy wakes to the sound of
> gunfire. Later in the day, while we sleep, this
> boy will leave his house and disturb a pile of
> trash meant for men in boots. It will explode.*

I will wake completely tangled up with this
child who snores and sleeps with his eyes
almost fully open. His bony feet kicking
mine, his head in the crook of my arm, his
elbows battering my ribcage. His sleeping
bag abandoned on the floor.

> *His pieces will be collected. His father may be
> called. Someone will tell his mother. If anyone
> is counting, the death will be registered. Will
> anyone ask his mother, "Did you kiss him before*

> *he left or did he sneak off to play in the streets*
> *while you were busy with ordinary chores?"*

I will disentangle myself, get up, grant
myself the slow luxury of French press coffee brought back to bed and read, my back
aching from a night of disturbed sleep.

> *No official report will record whether she felt*
> *a sharp pain the moment it happened, if she*
> *felt an immense, inexplicable grief when she*
> *heard the distant boom of the explosion that*
> *ended his life.*

He will laugh aloud in his sleep, and I will
touch my palm to his forehead and smile.

> *There is no tally of how many mornings she*
> *will wake and have to teach herself grief all*
> *over again, having forgotten in the night that*
> *the impossible has happened.*

When Zaki wakes and I tease him for snoring, he will say he was awake the whole
time. That he had been running security
all night.

Armor

Sometimes the barrier evaporates and my porous interior is exposed. People I love and work closely with, people who make my life more beautiful and bearable are suffering. People in the newspaper and on the radio. People I barely know have brought their suffering to my groups with courage and grace and honesty. I absorb it, grow heavy from it, sink to a depth where the pressure causes me to crumble. I don't know how to metabolize it.

I can't think of why I should do the things that usually seem so important—going to work or to the doctor or to dinner with friends. I will, of course. I will do all of those things. I will be penetrable and hold my face in a certain way that I have learned keeps my tears at bay. I will smile and make light conversation on the in-patient wards, I will go out and laugh a little less brightly, ask people who love me to carry me and hold me closer and tomorrow the film will settle over me and my focus will become soft again.

Beaches

My head feels full, uncomfortable, constipated. Like the urge to sneeze, the urge to cry rises then quickly passes. I can't seem to think about my impending divorce or my father's death for more than a few moments. To make myself cry, I decide to watch *Beaches*, a Bette Midler movie from the late eighties that always made me cry as an adolescent. The mother dies. The husband's a jerk. Bette Midler's character is sassy and triumphant. I send Marcus, my best friend at work, a text message asking if he'd like to join me for this experiment. He says he's never seen it and goes to Blockbuster while I work late. He gets the movie, buys tissues and popcorn.

We play the movie on the flat screen TV attached to the wall in his room in the barracks. We lay side by side on the twin bed, my head on a lumpy plastic pillow, his on a folded sweatshirt. Assigned to the Wounded Warrior Regiment, Marcus is responsible for between eight and twelve wounded Marines recovering here at the hospital. He checks on them every morning, mediates domestic disputes, gives them a hard time if they slack off on their appointments. He fights battles with doctors and case managers on their behalf and helps their wives and mothers navigate the complicated task of caring for a severely disabled loved one they've just been reunited with. Marcus himself has deployed several times in his more than a decade in the Marine Corps.

During the movie, Marcus's BlackBerry begins to sing with emails. When an active duty US Marine is injured anywhere in the world, an email goes out. At certain times of day, someone sits down and enters one report after another into the system, and Marines attached to wounded warrior units across the world get a stream of emails. He turns the phone to silent. We laugh at Bette Midler's plucky New York phrases, swear we're going to make them our own. We comment on the eighties outfits, I sing along to the songs. Marcus, uncomfortable with the whole enterprise after all, makes conversation during all of the saddest parts. The plan to cry fails.

There are dead cockroaches lining the walls of Building One when I get to work on Monday. Not just a few, but hundreds of them, crunchy red-brown bodies upturned and ugly, rocking in the currents generated by uniformed and civilian bodies rushing down the halls. If I were superstitious, I might consider this an omen. So much death: it's going to be a bad week. Or, humans versus nature, battle won: it's going to be a good week.

Building One, the original hospital, is a three-storied mass of brick sprawled in the center of the campus. It contains chandeliers, red carpets and exposed plumbing, Burger King, a barbershop, and a kiosk that sells counterfeit designer bags. An underground tunnel connects it to the new hospital, Building Two.

Major Hallow comes to my office referred by Alyssa, an acquaintance of mine who thinks Major Hallow might benefit from art. Major Hallow is a petite soldier in camouflage. She has a face like a doll: high cheekbones, long, curling eyelashes fringing big eyes. Dainty hands. She sits in a chair across from me at the worktable and I bring out beads. She has been an ICU nurse for eight years. She has worked in trauma and in the burn unit. She deployed to a combat zone once. Recently, her short-term memory has left her; she can't focus. She has been tested for traumatic brain injury and post-traumatic stress.

She tells me about a wounded warrior who had a prosthetic hip, leg, and half leg who went on a roller coaster after being discharged. He was sitting in the front car. *They must have cheered for him when he got on*, she said. *But then in the second loop, he was ejected. His prosthetic hip wasn't strong enough to hold him in. So he went flying out.*

Can you believe that? Her big eyes filling with tears from the bottom up, like a little bird in a cartoon. *He goes to war, gets blown up, survives and then dies on a roller coaster? It's ridiculous. And you know what his mother said to the newspaper? At least he died doing something he loved. Can you believe it?*

I've been saying exactly this about my father's death by drowning for a month now, so I *can* believe it.

Imagine how she feels, though, I remind her.

And what about the other people on the ride? Watching a wounded warrior plummeting 200 some feet to his death? I cry every day, she says. *The other day, I saw a quadruple amputee in the hospital. His wife was pushing a stroller with a tiny baby in it. He will NEVER hold that baby. By the time he gets his arms, that child will be walking. I cried. Now do you think that's what they need? Me crying? I don't even know what's wrong with me. Nobody knows what's wrong with me.*

Maybe there's nothing wrong with you, I suggest. *Maybe we should all be walking around this place bawling.*

Stones

Yesterday a man wrote a story about a bullet he wishes he did not have to fire but would not take back. I could feel grains of sand against my face. His voice hinged on tears only once in the telling, but the paper trembled between his fingers from the moment he cleared his throat and said, "I'll read." That bravery broke and remade me.

When I got to my office between sessions, I collapsed into my chair, feeling like little more than a pile of clothes. The social worker from across the hall, with scars on the backs of her hands from something she survived, walked in and said, "I've never been fired before."

I stood and offered her my arms, and she emptied tears onto my shoulder for a few minutes before taking her belongings, the cartoons she painstakingly taped to her office wall, and walking out.

And at my next session Delaney, who irritated me when he was a colleague in uniform, came to writing for the first time. He poured heavy stones of grief onto the table and they tumbled past everyone and came to a rest in front of me. And the thing is, I can't carry all their stones and no one stone is heavier than another and I wonder whether I busy myself with their stories so I can distract myself from the burden of my own.

If You Were a Demi-God

Athena of reason, of strength, of literature. Companion of heroes. Athena cracks through her father's skull, fully formed. She is never seen helpless, vulnerable, in need. Goddess of the loom weaving delicate, breakable strands into story, creating a holograph of meaning.

A woman who turned a lesser woman into a spider for saying she could defeat her.

What sweet smelling mortal did she succumb to? What words did he use to convince her to shrink to the size of an ordinary woman?

At which moment did she admit the limits of her surrender, realize that he would never understand her responsibilities to the children of war? When she stood, forearms still sticky with the juice of fruit from his garden, shaking flowers from her hair as she lifted the helmet back onto her head, when she returned to godly proportions, did she miss the simple task of sweeping cobwebs from corners with a broom?

I Woke This Morning
To Two Things

An article about four Palestinian boys killed at the beach. The oldest was eleven or twelve and had sent his eight-year-old brother home, because it was "too dangerous." In the interview with the reporter the eight-year-old child said, "He was always worried for me."

An email from Karim, wanting to discuss why our sons punch each other so much.

Instructions

Be brave. Do the things you are afraid to do. Do them alone.

Listen. You will learn the most before you've said anything about yourself.

Be patient. Do not dismiss anyone for a single act of unkindness. Remember how little you know about where they have come from. Remember that nothing anyone does is actually about you.

Be cautious. Not everyone has your best interests at heart. This is not paranoia.

Be kind. It is through kindness that you will scrub away at the surfaces of people and reveal how much they are all the same, how much they are all like you. It is through kindness that you will overcome your loneliness.

Be grateful. Do not take any smile for granted. No one owes you anything.

Be grateful. There are many other lives you could be living. There have been many opportunities for the life you are living to end.

Be grateful. At the end of the days when your hands are caked in paint and your heart is heavy with stories, know that you have spent the day wisely. Do it again tomorrow.

Why

This weekend someone asked, "Why do you care? Why do you care whether someone spends the weekend wallowing in their barracks room or eats dinner or sleeps or feels like shit? Why do you care?"

I've been asked *how* I care so much, which is different (and also unanswerable) and I've been asked how I *survive* caring so much (which I have a short answer and long answer for—though sometimes I just barely scrape by) but *why* is different.

Why is rooted in the fact that in every person I see a reflection of myself (good or bad) that I want to shield from suffering the way I want to be shielded. Maybe by saving you I can save some part of myself.

September 11, 2001

I was a stay-at-home mom and a part-time college student. I was out painting on the back porch with my toddler, living the isolated life of the American mother. My husband called and told me to turn on the television.

Soon after, I did the only thing I could think to do: I organized my first community event, an interfaith vigil in Rockville. The only way I could see myself or the people around me getting through this was by coming together, in spite of our differences, to share our grief.

It is through interdependence and grace that we can learn to care as much for one another as we care for ourselves. And to care for ourselves as much as we care for our children.

Your Work

Unless you have known the nights when you try a cup of tea, a second glass of wine, finish the whiskey, fill the tub. Will your heartbeat to slow.

Unless you have watched the hairs on your arms rise, seen little bubbles form on your skin, imagined filling your lungs with water and maybe sometimes you even bring your face to kiss the surface of the bath, sip it lightly with your nostrils, just to feel the warmth of it.

Unless you are aware that this is never about your funeral or *they'll be sorry*. This is about extinguishing the fire burning beneath the howling kettles of suffering you try to keep from boiling over.

It is about silencing the voices of mistakes you should not have made: the abortions you should not have had, the man you should not have married—should not have left.

The father you should have loved better before he died. Unless you have been there and have managed to escape you cannot understand that madness is at once temporary and chronic, a vine that withers and returns.

Your work is to keep an eye on it.

And no matter how many times you cut it back there is always the risk of another spring, a good rain, the required amount of shade pulling you under.

Things I Will Never Say
To a Group of Participants

Sometimes, when you look up from your paper shaking, I don't want to know. No matter how big the words in your poem, I'm never going to sleep with you. In almost every group, there's one person I hope never makes it back into the general population. I wish I could hug you, press the back of my hand to your cheek, compensate for your mother. Quoting Thoreau does not increase the odds that I will sleep with you. When it's just me in the room and the door closes, I'm supposed to be scared, but I'm not. I dream your dreams. I have learned the meaning of fear.

I
  don't
      know
         why
           you
              shouldn't   commit   suicide.

I Don't Know Why You
Shouldn't Kill Yourself

Tomorrow is the most terrifying day
of the week and even sleep, if it comes, leads you
unwilling, to stand in the ring on the packed red dirt
tired as you are of bowing and raising your heavy head
of putting on the show of stomping, of charging.

It *will* get better,
but the worst in your past vows to rise
in thick columns of smoke again and again
stinging your eyes and enveloping days.
Ahead lies paperwork, and consequence,
and more nights of gravity without ground

I can't promise you anything,
                              can't live for you,
                              can't quiet memory
or stem the flow of hot panic.

I can't tell you how many pills or poems until
the heat of this fever has passed
and you regain your taste for
the metallic sweetness of frosting dissolving on your tongue
the insides of eyelids turned amber by sunlight
the pleasure of noodles spooled around a fork
while outside rain falls

the way your daughter's laughter and tears burst forth
with equal sudden commitment

But maybe if you can train your grief to lay down by itself
after you gently rock it to sleep,
you can tiptoe away for just a moment
and then a moment more, to discover the lightness
that still exists in your outstretched arms
maybe you can begin to imagine another way
and find a reason not to do it today.

Mom

Years ago, someone said she'd never amount to anything, and she grew taller, traded in the peacock colors of high school for camouflage. She was not afraid to lose the things she knew—her father's never innocent touch, her mother's slurred words. She has gotten orders.

She puts her children to bed, but doesn't tell them yet, though she begins to say goodbye. Maybe they can feel her holding them tighter. She will keep them home from school on random days between now and her deployment. She will miss birthdays; she cannot be sure how many.

The other soldiers will call her Doc, they will call her mom. She will bandage them and remind them to stay hydrated and she will hold their intestines in when they spill from gaping wounds. She will see streets littered with body parts; she will tend to Iraqi children. She will bring their ghosts home with her. I will ask her what it is like to have kissed your children goodbye for maybe the last time, and then get to come back to them.

She will tell me she isn't back yet.

Same Shit

In a writing group, an OIF veteran asked an older veteran, *What did Vietnam smell like?*

He turned toward her, his back straight as the chair pivoted, and laughed for thirty seconds. A booming laugh, and everyone else in the room began to laugh too. *It smelled like war always smells. Like burning shit.*

Bad Guys

You think I'm good. I'm no good guy. He is clicking his pen, elbows on the table, his composition book open in front of him. He is the only person in my writing group today. He is tall, broad, with short hair and glasses that are tinted dark. He is kind and gentle and intellectual. He has done terrible things on his five combat tours. He is one of the best people I have ever met.

You want to know the truth about good guys and bad guys? He asks me. *There are no good guys. Only bad guys and other bad guys and innocent people caught in the crossfire.*

I think maybe there are only good guys, all caught in the crossfire.

Torpedos

I am throwing the orange rubber torpedo into the deep end of the swimming pool. It glides, then sinks, and my children splash to retrieve it, their slick black heads disappearing and surfacing.

A helicopter appears overhead, its cycles of sound beating like a pulse. As though the sky has unzipped and for a brief moment the clockwork has been exposed.

I watch its reflection pass from the disturbed surface of the water, which is so vividly blue I am amazed it doesn't tinge the boys' brown skin or the soft bright towels they wrap around their shoulders when they emerge reluctantly to step toward home, their wet footprints vanishing from the pavement behind them.

Cracks

Once I was held like a fish in a glass bowl with cracks that obstructed my view but couldn't be seen from the outside. Swimming in tight circles over pretty, artificial rocks that gleamed in the sunlight, I tried to recall a dream of open water. Afraid of what would happen if the glass broke.

When it broke, what caught me was the murky world, its stinging salt and terrifying depths, its uncertainty and questions and grays and blues unlike any dream. Here I met men and women, soldiers and poets and lovers who are willing. Some of them are newly sitting amongst shards of glass. Some have just gained the courage to hammer at the cracks. All of us lost and willing to find our way.

In Darkness

I wish I could show you, when you are lonely or in darkness,
the astonishing light of your own being.

—Hafiz of Shiraz

Greg is spelling words because I can't understand what he's trying to say. He speaks of himself in past tense—*I used to be a cool guy. I used to be very competitive.* His right hand is in a brace. Permanently. He is in a wheelchair, paralyzed from the waist down. He wants to do spoken word poetry. He wants to sing karaoke. He wants to start a band on the ward. He is working on a painting for his wife on a large canvas on which he asked me to trace his left hand again and again, an animation of waving. She doesn't visit often. They were barely married a year when he was injured two years ago. She is young. They both are. He asks me, as he painstakingly tries to get the peach colored paint within the wide outline of his hand, *Do patients ever annoy you?*

In a writing group in the partial hospitalization psychiatric program, the patients don't want to write. The restlessness in the room shuffles my worksheets, my careful lesson plan. *Let's write a list poem,* I say. *Tell me what you want to say to me.* One of the patients, a heavyset bald-headed man in Army PTs asks, *Do you know where the panic button is?* I do not. The man who asks is sneering at me, and I answer before I can think. *If one of you kirks out,* I tell him, *there are at least nine others who are itching for a fight—so I'm pretty sure*

I'll be okay. We all laugh, even the man who asked the question, and the cloud hanging over us floats a little closer to the ceiling. I feel many things, but afraid is not one of them.

Steven is leaving. He shows his new Veteran ID card with a big smile. It shakes in his hands. For months I held him like a found bird, ran my words along his brokenness, teased him about his diet and watched him unfurl, his laughter coming more and more easily. I want to tell him something that he can carry away with him. I want to fill his reservoirs with love, want him to take something that I gave him everywhere he goes. But there are no guarantees.

Todd is leaving next. He has been at the hospital for years, his health steadily deteriorating. He has a brisk way of solving problems, of helping a child tie a knot, pulling out a hunting knife at the art table before I can walk over and get scissors. *The things I have done in this uniform. I don't feel proud to wear it. I don't deserve to wear it.* Come next week he won't be authorized to wear it. I wonder how much of himself he will leave on the hanger with the uniform. I wonder who will call me when he dies by his own hand. I wonder how long after it happens I will find out. I wonder if I will feel the cord between us severed.

Carlos speaks of charred bodies, orders to fire, disrespect for the dead, Army failures, Marine Corps failures, terrorist failures. Red mist. His accent is thick; he wears a white sweatshirt and a gold cross on a thick chain lies over the crew collar. His eyes are wide, spittle flies. He is telling his stories insistently, as though we don't believe him. As if he himself cannot believe they are true. He is sitting eight or ten feet from me and I can feel the noise within him crackling through his skin, coming off of him in waves and when it reaches me I feel his shaking in my chest. I wonder if my taking has lessened his burden. Or if pain just multiplies.

Warnings For My Sons

The first time I read about the murder of Tamir Rice, a twelve-year-old boy shot by Cleveland police for waving a toy gun at a playground, I tell my sons, eight and fourteen, to pause the television. We are watching a show called Once Upon a Time, based on fairy tale characters who are dealing with the ultimate curse: reality. I read them the whole article, word for word, from the link I clicked on my Facebook feed. I read them Tamir Rice's father's words, "He didn't know what he was doing. He was only twelve."

They pay attention to my words in the way they do only when I am telling them something in this tone of voice—a voice I cannot fake—the scared quivering that sounds like a squint. We are cramped on the couch in the apartment we moved to when I left their father, our legs piled on top of one another. The television is paused on one or another fair-skinned, flowing-haired heroine. On this show, every rescue emerges from doing the easily identified right thing, every curse is broken by the everlasting magic of true love.

I remind them of the rules: no bomb jokes, no tossing around the word terrorist. No sending text messages that could be twisted against you. No buying those stupid dummy grenades you are fascinated by at the army surplus store. I tell them, "I don't want to scare you." But that's not true.

I have these conversations with them when I am afraid. When something happens in the news. When I imagine the black tops of their heads in the sights of a drone. As far as I know, the United States doesn't use drone strikes domestically. Our police forces are still struggling to figure out how to operate and store the volume of MRAPS and assault rifles and grenade launchers that have come from the Pentagon's surplus. "There are people," I warn my sons, "who will be afraid of you. You should be afraid of them."

I have dinner with a man who is wondering aloud why Bill Cosby's victims didn't come forward sooner. He brought pizza and we are eating it over greasy cardboard at my dining table. The boys are with their father. I try to explain to him what it feels like to be a woman. To be always weighing risks, gambling. *You catch more flies with honey*, we are told. But terrible things have sweet teeth too. We are taught to prepare ourselves, stay guarded, expect bad things to happen. And when they do happen, they will be our fault. Because we were warned.

It is an unusually warm day in November. We are walking by the chain link fence encircling a swimming pool near our apartment building. My eight-year-old says, "I could sneak in there easily." I grab his wrists, kneel to face him. "You never break the law," I tell him. I know he will break laws some day. Rebellion is a rite of passage, a way to lash out against the terror of standing on the precipice of the long work of fending for yourself.

A year ago, I asked a dear friend, a black poet in his thirties, when he noticed a shift in strangers' attitudes toward him. "When did you notice strangers stopped treating you like a cute little kid?"

"When I started going places without my mom."

Body

It is not about the baby. Wide eyes, round limbs, tiny fingers—babies are all the same. The drive toward motherhood is a lust for the intoxicating power of bearing a mother's smell; to be the expert on so specific a subject.

To know what another person needs, though he cannot speak it.

Stars

The mother is the gravitational force, the star the entire family orbits around. If the mother is fractured (which she almost always is—all of us are), won't each of our orbits be irregular? And if we do not acknowledge this brokenness, if we endure it under a shroud of silence, feeling it only in the murky sense of confusion that arises when our connections to our mothers are interrupted by hidden histories, we cannot understand even our own movements. The light of our mothers nourishes us, enters us. This energy is in the very fiber of our beings. Some of our demons are not our own. To name them, we must look to their source, to our mothers.

My mother stayed married to my father in spite of his flaws—irresponsibility, a quick temper, flaws she would name and name again. But she never made my sisters and I suffer through the challenges of a broken home. She never yelled back at us (my father was another story), never bothered going to battle over things like whether we were eating salad or cleaning our rooms. Her goal was to be liked by us. Liked best. I have long considered my mother's patience as a virtue far beyond my reach. This lack of patience is my primary failure of her and my children. I now wonder if perhaps this hesitation to discipline, to show anger, was something else altogether.

About six months after Karim and I separated, it occurred to me that my children were going back and forth between two homes in which they were distinguished guests. If each of us was trying to make each moment the boys spend with us a treat, who was feeding them vegetables? When I made the decision to be that person, I was met with angry resistance from my children. I must have trust in my place in my sons' lives, in spite of how angry my decisions may make them. I have no fear of my family opting out of my life—this is a gift both of my parents gave me. But my mother's father left when she was a teenager. He opted out. Every story she told about him was about her misbehaving and him showing irritation. Did she blame herself on some level for the loss? For his leaving? What then, did she feel she had to do in order to protect herself from further loss?

Pity

The first time I decided to have a second child, I was following convention. Our older son would be five by the time the new baby was born. It was time. My husband, Karim, was ready and so I agreed. I was ready to buy a new house, decorate a new room—maybe in pink. I was ready to be pregnant and eat more cake. But I was reluctant to introduce myself as the mother of two.

One child is okay. One child will fold himself into the backseat of a two-door coupe. But *two* children? Two children require more car, less living room, a big backyard. Two children suggest you're in it for good. It is harder to find babysitting, harder to have sex, harder to be *you* with two children. So I wasn't one hundred percent thrilled. Though I knew it was the right thing for my life. A decision Karim and I would not regret.

I was pregnant before we really tried. Before I had even laid all these thoughts out.

I was so *charmed* that he wanted another baby. And flattered, validated as a mother. He wanted another baby with *me*. So I was pregnant. And determined to take pregnancy in stride. I was twenty-four. Healthy. *Pregnancy is not a medical condition.*

We went on hikes and on long bike rides. I drank tea (caffeinated), gave piggy-back rides, went to concerts and the pumpkin patch. I didn't throw up. I didn't feel too tired.

I hardly felt pregnant at all. I went to prenatal appointments, prepared four-year-old Sam for the new baby. *A baby is great*, I told him. *A baby will make you laugh and be your friend. A baby will be the best thing that ever happens to you.*

He was sometimes skeptical, but mostly uninterested. I took him to hear the heartbeat for the first time. He held my hand and cringed when my blood was drawn and smiled shyly at the attention from the doctor and nurses.

Sam was at school when the first call came. Karim was at the kitchen table, repairing his glasses with a tiny screwdriver. I was flipping through a catalog.

The nurse said my AFP test numbers came out too high for my eighteen weeks. There was too much Alpha-Fetoprotein from the baby's liver in my blood. Something about a possible neurological defect.

Or maybe twins, I countered. *I read the pamphlet.*

She scheduled me for an ultrasound with a specialist forty-five minutes away. I researched AFP. Called my sister. Cried. Hyperventilated. Felt melodramatic for overreacting.

I didn't tell my parents—they had a vacation planned at the time of the test, and I hated to worry them for what would surely turn out to be nothing. Karim was starting his month long end-of-year use-or-lose-leave-time vacation the Friday of the appointment. It made sense to start the vacation by getting this cleared up. Everyone assured me everything would be okay. I agreed.

The doctor's waiting room was a bare rectangle. Walls lined with chairs upholstered in mauve. I was tempted to leap from chair to chair while I waited.

I was having twins! Or maybe my due date was earlier than the thus far predicted May. I filled out the form. A genetic Cosmo quiz.

Are you Jewish, Hispanic, over thirty-five? Are you and your spouse related? Do you have any history of genetic problems in your family?

We aced the test. All nos. Congratulations, you're having a healthy baby.

The waiting room began to fill. There was a Hispanic couple with a three- or four-year-old daughter. There was an older couple. Waaaay older. I felt sorry for them. I nudged Karim and whispered, *There must be something wrong with their babies. They must have failed the questionnaire.* He nodded in agreement.

We went in and met the doctor. Bald and unfriendly and delicate, he performed the ultrasound silently in the cramped, dark room. He didn't make small talk, didn't point out the baby's body parts. He kept the screen to himself. We thought he might have social problems.

He left the room (my belly sticky and exposed) and came back with a nurse in pink scrubs. She ran the machine. She left the room.

He came back. *The prognosis is not good.*

I was still smiling to encourage the doctor's social skills.

There's very little amniotic fluid. Terminate. Soon. You're young. Have another baby later. Are you leaking fluid?

I wasn't.

Your outcome won't be good, you have to decide soon. Before it's too late to be legal.

At some point, I dropped my smile, refused to accept it. Demanded a rematch with another ultrasound machine. They worked us into the schedule for Monday. We walked out through the waiting room, tears streaming. And the couples waiting must have felt so sorry for us.

The hours after you get bad news are like airplane turbulence. The weightless rise on the first impulse to convince yourself that you misheard, that the information was faulty. The grasping and scrambling on pure air. And then the down side, the drag: when you're yanked down from your gut and you just want to fold.

I rested my head against the cold window of the car, letting it bounce against the vibrating, buzzing glass. Karim drove fast, expertly, left-handed. His right hand was in my lap, enclosing my left hand, almost touching my rounding belly. Several times words formed in my mouth and when I released them, they bounced between us, as hollow as tennis balls.

My oldest sister, Mona, picked Sam up from school that first day. She had made beef stroganoff (my craving) and bought sparkling cider to celebrate the inevitable all-clear. When she answered the phone, I echoed the doctor: "The prognosis isn't good."

When I hung up, she called our parents back from vacation, called our aunt and uncle in Baltimore, put away the sparkling cider.

It was dark in her living room. Mona had recently moved, and the room was empty aside from an ornate bench and an opulent rug. I sat on the edge of the bench and dialed my aunt the pediatrician.

When she answered, I stood and traced the edge of the rug with clockwise steps. I told her what the doctor had told me and then answered all her questions.

The fluid is low. Five cc's. Eighteen weeks. High AFP. Dr. Khrusey. I'll have another sono on Monday.

She didn't offer her classic you-are-overreacting irritation, didn't explain how it was really not such a big deal. Just told me to prepare for a difficult journey.

I cancelled the follow-up appointment scheduled for Monday. I went to better appointments arranged by family and friends with prominent doctors; doctors with websites and publications.

We saw the beautiful doctor whose waiting room was packed full of pregnant women grumbling with discontent at Food Network on the television. When she performed the ultrasound, she turned a little screen toward me so that I could see as well. With the fluid so low, there was only gray, with the steady pulsing of a small heart in its midst. Then she held my hand and cried; she had lost a baby of her own just months before. Her nurse cried too. Karim kept his eyes wide and dry and asked questions.

We had another appointment after that, with Johns Hopkins doctors—*the best of the best*. The Hopkins doctors were narrow and intellectual and striking. They didn't wear make-up, didn't seem to brush their hair. They wore sweaters and socks of thick, practical wool with their scrubs. They gave us a jewel of hope and put me on light bed rest for a month. Karim gave a homeless man a twenty on the way home, succumbing to superstition after years of cocky agnosticism.

On bed rest, I watched every movie anyone recommended: *The Royal Tenenbaums*, *The Life Aquatic*. I fell asleep during *Star Wars* three times until Karim gave up. I wet the bed a few times, woke hopeful, and went to the doctor thinking the fluid leak mystery had been solved, that we might finally know where it was going.

While I was inert, a tsunami in South Asia caused hundreds of thousands of deaths and left families devastated. I avoided the news, but Mona was obsessed, so the stories reached my ears. Against my will, it put my woes in perspective, all these people drowning on land. But inside my body my child was withering, the amniotic sac clinging to its limbs like a plastic bag.

According to the Internet, some babies with oligohy-dramnios in early pregnancy do make it. The baby was active, that was unusual, surely a good sign. I was drinking bottles upon bottles of water. I lay on my left side, removed caffeine from my diet completely. Pomegranate juice was supposed to be good, and I drank a tart cup full every afternoon. I tried anything that was recommended. Except for God. *If* he existed, he was clearly overwhelmed.

After my month was up, I went back to Johns Hopkins. Nothing had changed; my baby was still alive, the fluid was nearly nonexistent. A decision might have to be made after all. During the ultrasound, the doctor found that the baby had a cleft lip and palette. That was the first solid thing wrong with the baby.

Before that it was the fluid, only the fluid and so many guesses on how the low fluid might affect the baby. The bladder appeared to be filling and emptying and 'practice breathing' was evident and we saw sucking motions and the baby was moving, moving. So it seemed like maybe the fluid was *their* problem, not ours. But the cleft lip and palette made three things wrong and miracles more elusive.

I underwent genetic testing. The testing rooms at Hopkins are cavernous, sterile cubes of gray. They rubbed iodine on my belly and in dim light punctured my abdomen with a long needle and, guided by ultrasound, led it into the placenta and pumped in and out. Hard. I welcomed the pain. Everyone was so nice, so compassionate. But I remembered the things I'd done wrong:

I hadn't been off the pill for long before I got pregnant (two weeks)

I had a couple of drinks (five weeks)

I had to stop to breathe during a tough bike ride (ten weeks)

I lost control of a fight with Karim (fifteen weeks)

I went to a concert in a smoky bar (seventeen weeks)

I was bad about prenatal vitamins (most weeks).

The apricot placental tissue was sucked into the syringe, and my uterus cramped. As the iodine was wiped from my belly and the lights were turned up, the doctor said:

"Take it easy today and back to normal activity tomorrow."

"No bed rest?"

"It didn't seem to help, so no."

Even the best of the best were giving up.

After putting Sam to bed, I brought the CD player from my bedside table into the bathroom and plugged it in next to the sink. I pressed play, turned the volume up, filled the tub halfway with warm water and climbed in. I held my breath and lay down face first, checking that my ears were fully submerged, balancing my weight on my folded elbows to keep the pressure on my belly minimal. The edge of the drain plug pressed into the top of my head. I could hear long notes of music playing through the water and the garbled lyrics. When I pushed myself up onto my arms, the air felt sharp against my face and neck, the music seemed too loud. So I took another breath and lay back down.

Seema. SEEMA.

I turned onto my side to see Karim kneeling at the side of the tub on one knee. I pushed the wet hair from my face and smiled at him.

He put his face in his hands and shook his head, then looked up. I could see white all the way around his brown irises. "Why?"

"Oh. Sorry." I realized what he thought he had walked in on. "I wanted to hear what the baby hears. There's not really this much fluid in there, but there's fluid in the rest of my tissue. I think the baby can hear me singing. I think it hears you too." I pulled the knob and hot water rushed into the tub. When the water level rose to the overflow drain, I raised my foot and pushed it off. "I'm not suicidal. Are you?"

He furrowed his brows. "No. Why would I be?"

"Why would I?"

Karim sat on the lid of the toilet. He gave me a half-smile through the rising steam and I missed him. I missed the crinkles at the corners of his eyes when he laughed and I missed hearing what he really thought. I missed his old confidence, his I-can-solve-anything attitude. I missed making plans. We scheduled only as far as dinner tonight, what movie we should watch next. Each unwilling to bring up the topic our lives spun around lest the other be reminded of it in a rare moment of peace.

I unplugged the drain. Karim passed me a towel and steadied me as I stepped over the side of the tub. I stood in front of him and he rested his head against my damp body.

I protected my baby—there wasn't any fluid there to cushion my movement. I walked slowly to avoid jostling. Karim suggested tying pillows around my middle. I laughed. He wasn't joking.

My cousin was getting married, so rather than risk slipping in heels, I ventured out to buy flat dress shoes, a first in my adult life.

In the mall I felt absurd, conspicuous. Like a bear posing as a person. I felt certain that someone would stop me and tell me that I should be home crying. Karim walked beside me, his hand at my elbow. Within fifteen minutes I bought my shoes and left the mall. Another first.

My mouth always tasted unwashed, my hair lay flattened on one side. Deep circles had carved space under my eyes, and my cheeks were swollen from so much unearned sleep. A fog clung to me. I donned silk, lipstick, jewelry. The reflection of the sequins on my clothes made me wince.

The wedding was held in a plush ballroom adorned with chandeliers, yards of tulle and vases of flowers set on pedestals. At any point, the doctors told me, I was likely to become a tomb. I hadn't felt the baby move for a day and a half by the evening of the wedding. I smiled in pictures, ate what was served, congratulated the happy couple—all the while moving through syrup. I avoided adult conversation, and when it found me, my responses were mumbled and peculiar. Karim spent the evening taking photographs of our nieces, nephews, and son. Each time our eyes caught, he tilted his head to the side and I shook my head.

And when finally, on the car ride home we played music loud and I felt distinct kneading against the inside wall of my abdomen, I was not entirely relieved.

We met with a genetic counselor. Her office had two tweed chairs for us to sit in. I noted the placement of the tissues. There were tissues everywhere these days. Everyone expected me to cry.

While she asked us about our families' medical history, Karim sat at the edge of his seat, jiggling his far leg. I couldn't feel it, but it annoyed me. We offered my grandmother's cancer, my father's thyroid, Karim's grandfather's heart attack and early demise. Karim offered an autistic cousin, which seemed to pique her interest.

She showed us a chart of neatly arranged tooth-shaped chromosomes and told us about trisomy 23 and Spina Bifida. She told us adoption was an option.

At home it was back to the Internet. We Googled cleft lip. It's not a big deal, it can be corrected. There'll be a little scar above the lip, but so? Cleft Palette gets trickier.

I drew my tongue across the roof of my mouth. The joint jutting out would be missing in the baby's mouth. So the baby wouldn't be able to drink milk without a feeding tube. Breastfeeding—my magic trick—would not happen. A chunk of my resolve broke off and floated away. We began to divide.

When you die, Karim would tell me, *I will have you cryogenically frozen.*

When you die, I invariably responded, *I will have you buried.*

In eighth grade, I told the class that I was pro-choice for everyone, but pro-life for me. In tenth grade, a friend of mine was on her second abortion. I hit the prayer mat, reaching out to a God I had been on the outs with for years. In eleventh grade, I took a pregnancy test in the girls' bathroom at school and was relieved to have no decision to make. The following year my grandmother, watching my trash can like a hawk, noticed that I hadn't had my period in two months. I used tampons, which she did not recognize. She offered to take me for a quiet abortion. In college I discovered science. I pored over the laws of chemistry. For once, it made irrefutable sense. I took astronomy, calculus, physics—with each course, guilt over my doubts lifted until I was finally free of God. And then this.

Everyone told me to pray. There is a special prayer, the *Istikara*, Muslims use to help make decisions. A specific Quranic verse is recited just before bed and the correct path is revealed in dreams. In short, have a nightmare and forget it. Have a happy dream, and go for it. I wanted to believe that if God wanted my baby, He would take him. That I just had to wait and it would all unfold. If I did lose the baby, we would eventually be reunited and I would see it take its first steps in heaven. But I had seen a fair bit of

His handiwork, and had no confidence in His thought processes. So the decision would have to be mine.

Karim and I discussed it gently, one of us retreating when the other became agitated. He brought me articles from the Internet—babies who had made it. I carefully highlighted the differences between their cases and ours. I was *not* leaking fluid, our baby was younger, my fluid was lower. I had pored over these same articles, had asked the doctors many of these questions. I pointed out that while *the doctors said the baby was going to die horribly and then he did* was not a particularly compelling or interesting story, it was probably the more common one.

The uncomfortable truth was that it was ultimately my decision. While Karim was pleading with me to keep his baby alive, I thought of the baby, gasping for air like a fish out of water. I thought of Sam, burdened for life with a younger sibling who wouldn't be a companion. I thought of Karim, already stretched, trying to juggle the added expense and stress of a very sick child. I thought of myself, consumed forever with childcare and destined for a ponytail and untamed eyebrows.

One day, between movies, my cousin and I happened upon an episode of Oprah. Her guest that day was Mattie Stepanek's mother. Mattie was born with muscular dystrophy and passed away just shy of his fourteenth birthday. His mother spoke of his last moments, the intensity of his pain, the deterioration of his body as his muscles distorted and twisted him from within, causing him to lose his hair and fingernails while she begged him to stay alive for her. She spoke of his amazing accomplishments, his poetry and speaking engagements and the lives he touched. She didn't regret a moment of it. All I could think of was Mattie's fingernails falling off.

When I finally made the decision, it seemed so sudden—they told me it was a boy, they told me he was starting to get clubbed feet, they told me there was no hope. Hope was starting to feel like a selfish luxury and so I succumbed. I wanted this over. I wanted to be with Sam, to make pancakes with him and enjoy his four-year-old wisdom instead of shuffling him from family member to family member. I wanted it to end.

I had seen all the pieces before—the low fluid ultrasound, the sharp, stark line of the needle as it enters the image on the screen. Though they turned the screen away from me, I could see it all. Karim watched the screen. He held my hand, but my guilt and his uncertainty made the motion feel automatic.

I wanted to shut my eyes, but I forced myself to look at Karim's face. His jaw was clenched, his eyes wet. The needle went in, full of adrenaline. I imagined it piercing through the soft, unformed fetal breastbone, entering the heart that I had seen pulsing rapidly at my first prenatal appointment, the heart that I had lain in examining rooms listening to.

Oh. The doctors (residents really—doctors are reserved for life saving) whispered among themselves briefly. They prepared a second needle.

It didn't work? I considered reconsidering. Was this a sign? Should I just get up and run, leave my shoes, my purse, my pants? In went the needle again, and this time it worked. Karim let go of my hand. I shut my eyes and they cleaned me off, turned on the light and began to tidy up. I put on my maternity jeans.

They led me down a long hallway with no doors. Behind me were the series of passageways that led to the ultrasounds, the examining rooms, the genetic counselors' offices. Before me, the nurses' station in the blue tiled labor and delivery ward shone.

Pulling a twenty-three week old fetus from the womb is not simple. First, a steady drip of Pitocin is fed into to the blood stream to induce contractions. One thousand milligrams of Tylenol are also administered to fight the inevitable fever that arises when the body resists relinquishing the baby. Next, to begin the dilation of an unwilling cervix, toothpicks of seaweed are forced into the tight tissue every hour or so.

I watched CNN during my first seaweed treatment. With studied focus, I read the ticker tape to the doctor and nurse, and we discussed current events like friends.

Karim stood by the bed, folding and unfolding his arms and staring at the television. When the doctor and nurse left the room, he sat next to me on the bed and I pressed my face into his neck. His warm skin smelled of home.

I felt the baby twitch and brought my hand to my stomach. *Rigor mortis?*

After a few hours, the Pitocin began to kick in. Another drip was attached, this time with morphine. The nurse handed me a button that would release the painkiller into my blood. My fever spiked and I began to vomit.

Mona, who had brought our mother along after arranging childcare for Sam and her own daughters, tied my hair back with a child's turquoise flowered tie pulled from the depths of her purse. My mother looked frightened and hollow. Karim held the kidney shaped bedpan under my mouth until I laid back.

I opened my eyes needing to vomit again. *Karim, the thing. I need the thing.*

The room was amber and blurred. I heard only shuffling and murmuring. They couldn't understand me, and

I growled louder, frustrated, my mouth felt full of rocks, my jaw twitched. The effort to speak exhausted me, taxed my diaphragm. I had a faint impression of the bedpan being passed from hand to hand until Mona or Karim or my mother was holding it in front of me. I retched and lay back.

Time passed. One nurse left, another began her shift. The contractions started to come. I still had not used the morphine. I was in control of that, swallowing the pain.

A few times I opened my eyes and the room was quiet. Two people had left the room and the third was snoring softly on the chair in the corner. I had nothing left to offer the bedpan, so I sat in the dark with my hands folded under my belly until sleep took me again.

As night began to give over to morning, the contractions came closer together. Karim had just fallen asleep, and I hated waking him. He stood and rubbed his eyes with his fingertips, disoriented. The shake of his head, the crush as he brought himself to the present made me fully conscious for the first time in eighteen hours.

This is usually the exciting part. He came and stood to the right of the bed, pressed the back of his hand against my cheek.

My sister and my mother stood behind him, near my head and I heard my sister whisper to my mother: *You can stay, but do not gasp.*

I pressed the button twice, ready for the morphine.

The gentle doctor who I had seen while I still held hope arrived. She and the nurse assembled in the room with a timid resident. The doctors stood at the foot of the bed, and the nurse stood to my left.

The nurse put her hand on my left leg and told Karim to put his on my right, as he had nearly five years earlier. I looked at the ceiling, pushed once, and hardly felt the baby's body pass out of mine. My mother gasped.

The doctors rushed him to the edge of the room, away from me, and the nurse began to massage my belly for the afterbirth. *Hardly any fluid at all*, she mumbled. And I was relieved.

My mother and sister left us alone. When the doctor brought him back to me, he was bundled into a hospital blanket, shrouded.

She gingerly peeled back the edges of the blanket uncovering his face, like flower petals. I was as eager to see him as I had been to see my live baby. His face was small, pointed, and beautiful, in spite of the cleft lip. As she transferred him to me, she explained that the right side of his body was open, had never closed.

The bundle was light, like a nightmare in which your baby has disappeared. But he was there, and when I pulled back the blanket to see his body, his inky purple intestines were spilling out of his right side and sticking to the cotton. His entire body was the length of my forearm.

I opened his mouth, gently pushing down on his chin with my forefinger. There was no cleft in his palate. The roof of his mouth was whole and joined. He could have been fed without a tube.

His tiny tongue lay neatly behind his lower gums, pinkish gray and pointed like a cat's. He had faint eyebrows and eyelashes. His eyes would not open. His hands were gummy and curled, his brow furrowed.

My mother returned with a croissant and attempted to force bites into my mouth. I turned my head away and golden flakes fell onto the receiving blanket enveloping the baby. I laughed hoarsely through tears. *Imagine when they do the autopsy. They'll find cafeteria croissant all over him.*

Karim took the baby from my arms, and my mother continued to feed me, both of us shivering with the laughter that comes too close on the heels of tears.

I held him one more time before the nurse came to take him. I kissed the tiny concentric swirl of fine hair on his cold, yielding forehead. And then he was gone.

Alone

In the months between babies, before the cells that would become Zaki came together and arranged themselves against the walls of my body, I experienced a loneliness I had never before noticed. A sense of being alone in my body. The gurgles and movements were alien, without origin, a clanging from a distant machine.

Responsibility

We were generations of women raising women—had no idea what it took to birth broad shoulders and weak stomachs.

If you raise a girl poorly, she's got no self-respect, uses her body like a bargaining chip, starves herself when she should eat, eats when she should be wearing her bathing suit in the sun. But poorly raised men have been wreaking havoc with force for more generations than I can count.

How much power does one wield in raising a person who is the inheritor of power? Who was I to have the responsibility of teaching a child to grow into a man, when his father is just a boy? When I was just a girl using her body as a bargaining chip?

Awake

Those months, while inside me his body became something I could hold, I waited. I took hot showers until the smoke detector alarmed. I lost hours staring out the window. I was trying to fall back to sleep after being woken by a nightmare.

When I was six months pregnant with Zaki, my parents took Sam and me away for a weekend. We stayed in a sparse one-room cabin on a little island where the Potomac River rushes to meet the Chesapeake Bay. It was Fall, the air was wet and cool and we walked on the hard sand holding hands. My mother and I, Sam and my father, stepping carefully over fallen trees in bare feet and long sleeves.

The wind blowing strands of hair on my swollen face. Hot, sweet tea sipped out of plastic cups. Me and my parents and Sam. The baby curled inside me. The river and the bay on their journey toward the ocean.

I couldn't take enough pictures, couldn't take the right picture that would capture the stark, complicated contrast of the dark, wet bark, the upended roots pointing toward the water and the gray sky.

a five-pound bag of flour
stretched to the volume of a
one hundred and twenty pound woman.
A wisp of smoke, a few strands of hair,

you are scarcely more than an idea

Saints

Isn't the mother required to be a saint? Isn't the child required to edit her memory of the mother to see her as such? You'd be hard-pressed to find a lukewarm Mother's Day card. Everyone's mom is without flaw, the best mom there is.

The mother endures unimaginable pain, makes great sacrifices, and delivers boundless, unlimited, selfless love. In return the mother receives loyalty. No adult tells the mother's secrets—children may make the mistake, but by adulthood, we are taught to see the virtue of the mother as a measure of our personal worth. It is in all of our best interest to bury the secrets of the mother. This pact is especially tight between mother and son. A friend of mine, a man in his late twenties, whose mother's own history of abuse cast a shadow over his childhood said, *You could say whatever about Dad, you could argue with Dad. But say one thing against Mom and you'd get backhanded. By Dad.* If Mom does wrong, you look away. You do not speak of it; it is a matter of chivalry and family honor. The mother is perfection, all things good. The mother is not a person, she is an idea. Because her virtue and the respect given to her is tied so completely to her role as *their* mother rather than as a woman or mother in general, the exploitation of other women and girls is unimpeded by this classification.

Carol Gilligan writes, *To love freely, one must be able to experience one's feelings. And anger is just that—a feeling.* This quote is written in dry erase marker on the sliding glass door in the living room of our apartment. A lot of the reason I feel so completely destroyed by the occasional cruelty of my sons is because of my own insecurities around whether our relationship is "good enough," whether my commitment to them is good enough. I have long stretches of time away from them, during which I question every decision I've made as their mother, but also enjoy the limited responsibilities I have: the selfish way I can eat an avocado over the sink for dinner, drink a glass of wine and go to bed early or stay out all night with a man they will never meet. And during these absences, they feel abandoned and hurt, but also enjoy their father's household, the space to play, the video games and large television, the bigger budget for eating out. This is the private truth of mothers and children: we sometimes feel hindered and failed by each other, we sometimes prefer to be apart.

Driving

Marriage is war, I tell my sons. I have recently concluded a shouting match with their father. At a stoplight, I turn and look at the two of them strapped tightly into their seats. They look back at me with cartoon baby eyes. They have been through this before. They are not particularly alarmed. They are quiet, waiting.

The sun is shining, the weather is cold, I remembered my gloves and my house is clean. Today I am not weepy. I am jaunty, free, maniacal, confident. I am righteous and my vision is clear. Everything will be fine. Even if I married poorly, even if I don't quite know where we're going to go today. I have successfully shaken off his mood, have driven away from his voice while he bellowed behind me, and I will be fine.

Feelings

I picked Zaki up after eight days together and two days apart. I was taking him to a Halloween party and he stomped to the car, snapped at me, stood with his arms folded, wouldn't hug or kiss me hello.

Tell me what's going on, I pleaded. *Tell me what you're feeling.*

He refused.

You can't act like this with me every time. Remember how great it was, just days ago? What happened? I cried.

He cried, stared angrily out the window on the drive home.

When we got home, he screamed at me about the location of his favorite T-shirt and I screamed at him for screaming at me, when I am so good, when my own life is so hard.

I poured some plantain chips into a plain white bowl and we ate them standing by the kitchen counter, making apologetic small talk. The mood seemed to have passed.

Hey, why are you so rude to me when we first see each other?

He shrugged.

Do you act like this with Baba?

He shook his head.

Why do you act this way with me?

You are the only place I can use my feelings.

Bedtime

I am tired, I have too many things to do. I have taken them to the pool or to dinner, have watched a movie or played video games and the evening has crept by. I need to set the timer on the coffee pot and I need to make the sandwiches for tomorrow and I want to drink a glass of wine.

I have sung to them, have scratched their backs, have kissed their cheeks and have read a story or a poem. I have turned the fan speed up, have gotten another blanket, have tucked Sam's sheets in around him. I have gotten Zaki one more sip of water. I leave the room. Sam shouts out. Zaki is humming. They can't sleep.

Through gritted teeth I remind them that my patience is a finite thing. I agree to let them sleep in my bed. They argue over who sleeps on which side. Sam lays diagonally across the bed, his feet overlapping Zaki's legs. Zaki sticks a finger into Sam's belly button.

They complain about the fan speed and blankets in my room, where they insisted on sleeping. I rectify the situation, and leave the room.

"Your air-conditioner is making a weird noise," Zaki calls after me.

I return to stand in the dark room. "That's because you stuck things in it."

Sam laughs. "That's awkward."

Zaki giggles. I relax a little, kiss them one more time. I scratch their backs briefly. They take this opportunity. "We can't sleep. We never go to sleep this early at Baba's."

"That's fine," I tell them. "Don't sleep. I don't care if you just lay there all night. I don't care if you never sleep. I just don't want to see or hear from either of you again until morning."

The following evening they are back with their father. I wander the apartment like a ghost, waiting for an appropriate time to go to bed.

February 13

The night before you were born, I lay in the bathtub on my side, too swollen with baby to be submerged. Your father sat beside me, awake with us both, pouring cups of warm water over the loaded barrel of my belly. That kind of love is where the roots of this family are. And it is our work to convince you—and to convince ourselves—of the irreconcilable truths:

> *love like that existed once*
> *and we are all somehow better off now.*

Birth

When I was twenty-five years and nine days old, I went into labor for the third time. At the hospital, the nurses strapped an elastic band around the expanse of my belly, holding contraction and fetal heart rate monitors in place while I lay on my left side.

"I think it's time." I told the nurse.

She glanced at the strips of paper printing out reports from the monitor. "Not yet."

I had never gone this far into labor without the velvet of medication, so I wasn't sure. I had never felt something so outside of myself, beyond time or reason take hold of me. I wasn't sure. It continued. I vocalized through the waves of contractions, the nurse shushed me. The anesthesiologist was called in to pull the drapes down over my voice. He sat on a stool behind me, attempted to force his thick needle into my spine. In front of me, the father of my child attempted to hold himself steady. I shut my eyes. The anesthesiologist warned me to hold still. I heard a crash and opened my eyes to see the IV bag swaying on a pole where Karim had been. The anesthesiologist rolled his stool back. Someone brought a wheelchair, I turned on my back.

"Leave him," I said. "I'm pushing."

"Oh no, don't push," The nurses said to me.

"Catch this baby or don't."

She almost didn't. The anesthesiologist was in the corner, packing up his kit when my son was delivered. When my obstetrician finally arrived, my baby was nursing for the first time. Karim was having his head examined in the ER. I was lucid, un-medicated, euphoric on the tide of postchildbirth hormones.

"You could have done this by yourself," the doctor said.

Frogs

Zaki is sitting toward the back of the bathtub. In the front, near the faucet, two fish-shaped candles float in the remaining froth of bubbles. Zaki takes a bath nearly every night that he spends in my apartment. The bathtub will only seem spacious to him for a short time, and I want him to take advantage of it. He resists, but the promise of floating candles in the tub convinces him. I sit on a small step stool beside the tub, my arms folded along the white porcelain rim, the point of my chin pressing into the back of my hand. This red step stool was bought years ago to match the red of the kids' bathroom in their father's house, where I used to make decisions about wall colors and shower curtains. We are practicing our mind reading skills. One of us thinks of a number while the other tries to guess it.

"The frogs miss you." Zaki's eyes shine in the candle-light. He sits as still as he can, trying not to make waves that will drown the candles. His hair is laced with bubble foam. In the sepia light, the moment feels like it is already a memory. The frogs were a gift to the children from their father's cousin.

"How do you know?" I ask him.

"I can read their lips."

"What do they say?"

"They say, 'We wish she had stayed.' They don't know your name."

We wish she had stayed. I want to climb into the bathtub and embrace him. I want to explain that I didn't leave, that I am right here. Instead I tell him I miss the frogs too.

My Body

When you are slipping and seek something to grasp, remember the ledge of my clavicle. Never fall without a fight.

When you long for shelter, remember the threads of my fingers woven into yours. The web we made and remade.

When obstacles in your path loom large, remember my lifting grip under the hinges of your arms.

When you must endure without being overcome, remember the firm line of my forearm, the sticky hook of my elbow.

When your sorrow's clamor cannot be ignored, remember the scoop of my palm pressed to your ear, the dignity in surrender.

When you need a place to rest, remember the soft landing you found in the flat between my shoulder blades.

Riddle

You can't get him to brush his teeth, stand still while you talk, stop biting his nails or the collar of his shirt. You resort to the guilt trips and tears of your mother, because the embrace of your approval is no longer enough.

When he is in the best of moods, he asks you riddles: *What weighs more—a pound of feathers or a pound of lead?* He is astounded when you know the answer.

Better At a Dinner Party

Something had woken us, an errant alarm clock, a phone call from another time zone—I don't remember what exactly, but Sam and I were awake, and felt as if we'd had our fill of sleep. Zaki was still snoring in bed, mouth open, arms flung wide, the sweet round of his cheek pressed against the mattress.

I turned on the lamp, a tangle of Christmas lights hung on a hook in the living room, made cups of tea and we went out on the balcony to sit on the secondhand futon we keep out there. Just Sam and I bundled under blankets we pulled from the couch, existing in this sliver of time not allotted to any task, the sky lightening.

It was so early the stars were still out and we listened to the radio, heard a quote from Scottie Fitzgerald about her parents being *people you should sit next to at dinner parties, not live with*, and Sam looked at me and laughed and laughed and leaned closer and I felt like maybe all my oddness was a gift I was giving instead of a wound I was inflicting.

Magic

I was driving the children home one evening and Zaki asked me, *If you went to Hogwarts, what house would you be in? Are you brave or are you smart or are you unspecial?*

I said, *Unspecial.*

He said, *No. You are brave and you are smart.* They agreed that I wouldn't be a prefect because I'd get in too much trouble for pranks. As though these were the facts. They were not asking for ice cream or chocolate, not asking favors of me.

They could tell me that they hate me (they have) or that all their hardships are my fault (they have) or that I am getting pudgy and should jog (they have told me this too); but they never worry that I might turn on them, might stop answering their calls.

Sons

This morning as my sons got into the car ahead of me, I had a sudden, throat constricting realization that their limbs are lengthening and soon beards will start growing and there are people in the world who are already afraid of their names.

Sometimes Zaki needs to sit in my lap and cry while I hold him and even when my arms are no longer big enough to encircle him and my legs aren't strong enough to bear his weight, he will be my child, just as all men are somebody's son.

Pain

Yesterday Sam fell down the stairs at school. I was on a field trip to an art museum with a group of patients an hour away in Baltimore when Karim sent me a text message. I hurried everyone onto the bus and back to the hospital I work at, then got in my car and arrived at the civilian hospital in town as the nurse was slowly suturing a line of twenty-seven x's just under his kneecap. Karim and Zaki were standing beside Sam. The curtained-off area of the pediatric emergency room was the smallest space the four of us had inhabited in years.

Today, I have left him at home. Zaki—out of school for a teacher workday—will run little errands for him. I left money for pizza. It is Friday, and I have two sessions, a morning writing group and an afternoon drawing session. I will set up the afternoon session and leave the participants to their own devices, then go home and belong fully to my children. I will make dinner, place my palm on Sam's head and ask him again and again if he is okay, although I know he is fine.

Only one person shows up for the drawing group, a soldier in his early twenties I have been working with for eight or nine months. He had surgery earlier this week, and his neck is immobilized in a brace. I begin a project with him, drawing postcards with scenes from Greek mythology made modern. I want to make him laugh. He has been struggling with depression, but today it is compounded with post-op pain and is almost contagious. I am trying to think of how to extricate myself to get back to my kids, a part of me in motion although I'm sitting still.

Seema, he says in his long, slow way. *I'm in a lot of pain.*
   Do you need help reaching your meds? I ask him.
   No. My mom came for my surgery.
   That's good. He has a troubled relationship with his mom, and there had been some question as to whether she would show up for the surgery.
   When she left, she took my pain meds with her. I can't ask for more without getting her in trouble.

Oh man. That sucks. There is nothing else to say. I'm sure he could score meds off of someone else in the barracks, but that's definitely not what I'm going to suggest. Instead I settle fully into my body, give up any hope of leaving early. My work now is to hold this table steady for this woman's child.

My children cannot compete with this. When I get home, they will not understand.

Prophet

after Katie Regan

When your mother is a prophet
she gives endless chances to those who have killed and raped
and used and has no patience
for dishes left on the table or laundry scattered
on the bathroom floor.

She forgets to check your homework but expects only As
cannot understand why you want to kick a ball,
watch movies, read the same books again and again.

You explain to her about football
and she explains that life
is really about things you can't see.

When your mother is a prophet
she returns home reeking
of sorrow and cigarettes,
envelopes you for a moment,
kisses your cheeks, folds you into her arms.

She does not mean to rock only you.

Her love is so generic
you can hardly find yourself in it.

When your mother is a prophet
she works rituals into the unused edges
of life—steaming milk in assigned cups
dotted with marshmallows in the morning,
big dinner on Sunday evening
She starts to read aloud from the Odyssey
asks you to take over
because her throat is sore
when she tries to sing to you at night
you ask her to stop, because you

don't want her charity.

She tells you how much she loves you
but you are not convinced.

When your mother is a prophet
she drinks a glass of wine after turning
out your lights, then sinks into her bed
heavily.

You wait for her breathing to deepen,
then slip under the covers beside her,
catch the unconscious scraps of her affection.

She holds you tight,
slips lower until her head is on your chest
so that you can hold her.

When your mother is a prophet,
she stands at the stove and tears stream down her face
you cannot tell if you cause them.

You spend afternoons in
the dark deserted wing of a hospital

protected by armed guards,
packing artwork that frightens you
and represents her time away
and the people whose hands she holds
instead of yours.

When you see her among her devoted
they clutch her hands and tell you
what a marvel she is and you feel proud
and marginalized
by the way she tilts her head,
smiles humbly and returns the compliment.

They act as if they know you, they have heard
so much about you, are so glad to meet you and
you wonder if they would recognize
the woman who
narrows her eyes,
loses her temper, screams
like a shrew when she throws your cell phone
across the room because you are defiant

because you will not tell her
how you feel.

When your mother is a prophet she is frustrated
that you are not devoted,
that she can't use her canned sorcery to get you to see
how much she is doing, how special she is.

Hagar

Like Hagar, I leave my children in the sand in search of water.

I leave them with their father. Though he has shown he is capable of it, I trust he will not offer them up to the altar of his anger.

I wonder if the woman who has appeared by his side is the lamb who will be sacrificed in their stead.

Security

I make thrifty meat purchasing decisions at one end of the freezer aisle while Zaki window shops for ice cream at the other end. I hear him tell two children bickering in a cart, *Can you please stop being so annoying?*

Their mother's mouth falls open and she looks at me. I apologize, pull him towards me.

In the car, I tell him we cannot always just say the things we think. *What if their mom got so mad and wanted to fight me?* I ask him.

Oh, he says. *We would be right there with you, Mama. I would do anything for you, even sacrifice life.*

Bed

The rising sun is framed by the curtain-less window directly across from the king-sized bed Karim demanded I take with me when I moved. Most days, I rise with the sun, to the luxury of a coffeemaker that brews on a timer before I wake. I stumble from bed and pour myself a cup of coffee and watch the sky lighten until it is time to rouse the children. I go into their bedrooms, where Sam sleeps like a child in a picture of how children sleep—tucked into his bed, the blankets smooth around him. Zaki sleeps facedown diagonally on his twin-sized bed, the sheets tangled and wrapped around his body and wakes with the lightest touch and the promise of hot chocolate. Sam requires shaking and rough kissing on the cheeks.

They make the move to my bed. Sam slides deep under the covers facedown—most mornings he refuses the milky-sweet coffee he is partial to or the marshmallow-heavy hot chocolate his brother drinks religiously, the cup always tilted to the verge of tipping onto the white sheets. We listen to the voices on the public radio station and I drink my second cup of coffee. When the poem of the day comes on, I shush Zaki's slurping and Sam's rustling of the sheets to sigh along and repeat the lines I want to carry. I push off the covers and we begin our day.

Misery

I put the kibosh on video games for the weekend and the kids were pissed—folded arms, eye-rolling, exaggerated sighs every time I spoke to them. They were so pissed they were hell-bent on being miserable. They were so hell-bent on being miserable, they almost succeeded. But they didn't, because there's too much to enjoy. Even when you're fourteen and no one understands you. Even when you're eight and it seems like your mom is hardly ever around and when she is she's obsessed with vegetable eating. The lesson that I keep having to teach them (and myself) is that the decision to be miserable and the effort it takes to uphold that decision will almost always cost you more than it costs anyone else. You don't ever have to engineer misery. Misery is a single-celled organism that lives in all of us, threatening to divide.

Beyond

A large man with incongruously thin legs, my father's splayed steps were never more steady and certain than when he entered the ocean. Holding hands, we'd comment on the temperature of the water and what we'd be looking at if we could see the opposite shore. The goal, he said, was to get *beyond* the waves and swim on the other side. His grip on my hand never seemed quite tight enough; his large, soft palm felt like it could slip away, distracted, at any moment. But when the water got deep and the waves came pounding at my chest, knocking me over, his grip tightened and I folded my knees, forcing him to pull me up, to bear my weight. And he would laugh and continue walking, his stride unbroken, while I floated along beside him.

Soil

*Grief grows backwards: instead of
pushing upward, it recoils in upon itself, going from a bright green shoot to
a fuzzy, germinating thing, nestled in
the soil of the self.*

Storms

I dream now of storms. Rain falls in sheets; white trees of lightning illuminate a pitch-black sky. My chest hums from the vibrations of the thunderclaps, but I feel safe. I am at work, walking from my parked car, holding a black umbrella just big enough to shield me. I am unhurried, and a man I want to kiss waits under an awning in front of a metal building. I can't see his face. All night, I dream this dream, wake up and fall back into it. The storm rages. The man takes out his keys. I walk with sure strides toward him. At five-thirty, at the first buzz of my alarm, I get out of bed and turn on the light. I sleep alone now. Karim has vacated our bedroom, sleeps instead in what used to be the office in the basement. Our king-sized bed is just mine now, a luxury I usually enjoy. Today I wish someone were here to hold me.

I go into the bathroom and rub my eyes. My phone rings, showing a peculiar, very long number—someone far away. I tend to ignore unfamiliar calls like this, but I am grateful that someone somewhere wants to talk to me at this odd hour.

Hello? My rough voice echoes against the bathroom tiles.

Seema?

It is my mother. She sounds very, very small.

Yes, Ma. How are you?

Seema? She asks again, her voice getting stronger. *Seema? Abba died.*

Shut up, I say, smiling. *You're kidding. This is not funny.*

Seema. Why would I make this up?

Where are you?

In India, she says. *We had come to Fort Kochi, in South India, on a trip. Abba went for a swim, we were leaving today. He didn't come back. I waited for hours. And then the police called the hotel. He drowned.* The words come across oceans, over masses of land, one by one, robotic.

One last dip, I say. It was a ritual for my father. On the last day of a beach trip, he had to have one last dip in the ocean. *What am I going to tell the kids?* At this, I begin to sob, then abruptly stop. *Do I have to tell them? Can't we just not tell them? He could just be on another trip. Until they're a little older. Sam is only eleven, Zaki is just five. The divorce is so hard on them, life is so hard on them already.*

But my mother will not agree. I navigate the slowly lightening house to get to Karim; I wake him and tell him. He believes it immediately and puts his arms around me. This feels so good that again I feel perhaps lies are okay. *Do we have to tell the kids?* I whisper.

He nods. But I don't have to tell them immediately. I sneak off to work, the children still unconscious to the newest change in the landscape of our family. I ask Karim to take them to school. At work, I fill out bereavement leave forms, pass off work to colleagues. I tell acquaintances in the elevator that my father died this morning, to feel the words on my tongue. I am aware of their awkwardness, aware that this is a weird thing to do, but I don't stop myself. I go to the deli and get three sandwiches, three bags of chips, three chocolate bars, and Gatorade.

I pick the kids up from school early, before lunchtime. They come out of their classrooms bewildered, shielding their eyes from the sun with their lunchboxes. The sun is beating down viciously already; the humidity in the air makes everything heavy. I steady myself, make my eyes bright. I smile and tell them, *We're going to the riverside for a picnic.*

They are thrilled. *Is it a special occasion? Were we especially good?*

You're always good, I respond. This is not at all true, and they shift uncomfortably in the backseat. *Well, this has nothing to do with that. I just wanted to talk to you by the river.*

They are satisfied by this and the conversation wanders as we snake along the hilly roads that lead to the park. We pack the picnic into a cloth shopping bag pulled from the trunk and begin the familiar hike across the bridge over the C&O canal and through the entrance into the wooded trail that follows the Potomac River. Here in the shade it is easier to breathe. Sam spots a snake and we bend over to peer at it, our heads close. I put my hands gently on their small backs, feel their spines protruding through their damp T-shirts. They are so fragile, so human and alive. We continue to hike.

You know, I always come here when I'm sad. It makes me feel good to be in nature and feel small and a part of something bigger than my own life.

Sam turns to look at me quizzically, one eyebrow raised. He quickly faces forward and continues, faster now. Zaki says, *Yes, nature and especially trees, are much bigger than you. You are kind of small for an adult.*

The trail is broken by tree roots and rocks and Zaki is a distracted hiker who trips often. Sam is far ahead of us. *Let's go to our spot and see how high the river is right now*, I call to him. *Can you remember where the entrance is?*

He nods and slows a little. When he gets to the entrance to the little side path that will take us to the river, he waits.

The canopy of trees stops rather abruptly at this point, replaced by tall grasses and thorny bushes. The drone of water dwelling insects is louder, and the river is just a few yards away, making its own music. We leave the dim, sheltered path for harsh unfettered openness, making our way to the water's edge. It hasn't rained in a few weeks and the water level is low. We sit on the large, smooth boulders closest to the water and I pass Sam his sandwich packed in wax paper and unwrap Zaki's before handing it to him. Sam holds his sandwich, still wrapped and looks at me expectantly.

I close my eyes for a moment and then open them again. I look at Sam. His chin is starting to tremble; he can feel the bad news coming. This is the last moment of his childhood. *Nani called me this morning—*

No! Not Nana. Not Nana. Sam's face has crumpled, tears mingle with the sweat on his face. Zaki is sitting on his rock, observing. His face is mostly obscured by the giant turkey sandwich between his hands. He looks from Sam to me and back again.

Sam returns his sandwich to me, takes a deep breath, crosses his arms. *What happened?*

We're not sure. He went swimming, they were on vacation and we think he might have had a heart attack while he was in the water.

I want to go home. Right now, Sam says, ignoring my outstretched arms and turning toward the path.

Zaki hands me his sandwich and stands up too. I drop it all back into the bag and follow behind them. *You know, Sam*, Zaki says, scrambling up behind his brother. *These things happen all the time to lots of people. Even Max the dog, our neighbor, died.*

Shut up, Zaki, Sam growls back, picking up his pace.

I put my hand on Zaki's shoulder and give him some Gatorade to drink. *You're right, these things do happen a lot.*

Sam is further up the path now, and Zaki wipes his mouth with the back of his hand. *It should be that when you die, you're only dead for a day and then you come back. That would be better.*

Yes, it would be.

We continue up the path, and find Sam squatting beside a tree. He holds his hand up to stop us as we approach. He puts a finger over his lips and then motions for us to proceed. *It's a frog*, he whispers.

The little brown frog is blinking at the base of the tree, each breath making its tiny body quiver. Zaki leans forward, hands on his knees, and when he can no longer resist, he reaches a hand out to touch the frog. It hops away, navigating fallen leaves bigger than itself. We continue along in silence. Once in a while, Sam points to something beautiful as he passes it, but does not wait for us to examine it with him. He walks steadily on. When we emerge from the trail onto the towpath, Sam is skipping rocks in the canal. The towpath is gravel, so there are plenty of rocks to throw. In the interest of conservation, I usually place a limit on this exercise. Surely this gravel comes from somewhere and must be replaced. Today, I sit cross-legged on the path and allow them both to throw rock after rock into the water, watching the circles ripple outward as the rocks sink.

Voices

My first understanding of marriage: the sound of my parents' Urdu, their voices creaking in the pale white light of early morning. My father's glasses off, his eyes small, the hood of his eyelids, the shortness of his eyelashes, the masculinity of his face revealed. My mother's face pillow-creased and round, she holds a teacup in her elegant, unmanicured hands, her shiny black hair loose and tucked behind her ears.

In his endeavor to convert my mother to early rising, each morning my father brought two cups of sweet steaming black tea with milk, spilling brown over the edges of the cups to their bedroom, they would sit side by side in bed, propped up against pillows, talking quietly until my father's easy temper and my mother's sharp words awakened and the chores of the day ahead separated them.

Driving

My mother does not drive. She lived in the United States for more than thirty years and never learned to operate a vehicle. She can't ride a bicycle either. After I told her about the divorce, our telephone conversations shrank to idle chitchat. She called to ask what the kids were learning in school, what I'd cooked for dinner, and to tell me how each individual in our extended family was doing. She did not ask how I was feeling or what the next step would be. I called her on it one day.

I'm in denial, she said, as if this honesty would absolve her of weakness. Pressed further, she blurted, *This will ruin your children's lives. There is nothing worse you can do to them.*

I decide to avoid rather than deal with her. For the first time, I don't speak to her for months. Instead, she rides along like a ghost of judgment as I navigate my new life. When I sit in a bar flirting with an older, powerful man and he leans in and runs his fingertips along my bare arm. When I climb into a taxicab in the middle of the night with four Marines. When I am speeding down the highway on a rainy night travelling far out of my way to see a friend who is more than just a friend. I think of her, and I feel a shiver of loneliness. I am not who she thought I would be.

When The World Breaks Open

"In a way," Sam says, "I'm glad we have Zaki. He's so much stronger than me." We look over at Zaki, with the last cling of baby fat on his chin, sleeping with his eyes and lips slightly open. He begins to snore almost as soon as he's unconscious. Sam has come to my bed in this Virginia Beach hotel room, unable to fall asleep. He looks up at the ceiling, dimly lit by the pool lights coming in through the sliding glass door. "Why am I so afraid?"

"Well, what are you afraid of?" I ask him.

"Bees. Fires. Buildings collapsing. Nana's body coming to haunt me. Dying."

I remember his toddler fears of remote control cars, dogs, the ocean. I see that little face, a blurred, softer version of this eleven-year-old face, and I put my hand on his forehead, pushing his thick black hair up.

"I think you're afraid because that's your personality. Like my sister or your father. You think of all the things that could possibly go wrong. What you have to do is weigh the odds: a bee sting will be uncomfortable, sure, but what are the odds it will kill you? That you have a bee allergy? Very slim. So be cautious but don't be too afraid. Fires and building collapses happen, but again it's rare. In this situation, we are in a hotel with sprinklers in each room. So even if someone started a fire by accident, the sprinklers in their room would put it out. Nana's body haunting you . . ."

"Impossible," he says. "I know." He turns to face me.

"Well of course. But hard to forget, too." I pause, and remember the white gauze around my father's head, wrapping his forehead until two inches above his eyebrows. I see his darkened lips, flattened nose, the circling flies, the smell of formaldehyde mingled with attar. "You have to understand, his body was like that for a simple reason: bodies can't be left without blood running through them for very long. They need to be buried. Like if you took a bite out of an apple and left it on the counter. It would turn brown, wouldn't it? It's the same thing."

"That makes sense," he says. "I didn't think of it that way."

These are the words I needed, to calm me. Until now I have felt like I'm faking it, pushing motherhood to its limits in this conversation, on this trip. But finally I know that I have some of the right words. I face the final fear. "What about dying scares you?"

He thinks for a moment, turns his gaze back to the ceiling. His eyelashes are unreasonably long, like a camel's. His father's family hailed from the Indian desert several generations ago, and Sam's eyelashes are designed to handle a sandstorm. "That when you die, that's it. There's nothing more, it's all over; it's all dark." He adds in a softer voice, "I'm kind of afraid of the dark too."

This I can answer. "You don't have to believe that there's nothing more. That's what I believe, because that's what gives me comfort. But some of the smartest people I know believe in heaven and a whole other life after this. You can believe that if it makes sense to you, makes you feel better." I put my arms around him, kiss his hair, pull him close. "I don't think any less of anyone who believes in that stuff. I won't think any less of you for sure."

We are on our first trip, just the three of us. Virginia Beach is a four-hour drive from home. I have needed to make this pilgrimage to the ocean since my father's death. I book a hotel, put gas in the car, load a bag of clothes in the trunk and a bag of snacks into the passenger seat. I remember my parents' travel credo: for international travel you need only three things—ticket, passport, money. For domestic travel, all you need is money.

The hotel is more ragged than it looked in the pictures online, and the lobby and carport are teeming with vacationers of all ages and ethnicities. I find myself a parking space and get our luggage loaded onto a cart. We drop our bags in the room, change to bathing suits and head directly to the swimming pool.

For the first time I don't feel sad about families I see. I don't even notice the absence of that sadness for hours. This is progress. I can sit by the pool and hear a man ask his wife what she wants to drink and feel no envy. The envy may return some day, but today I feel like a badass. I am here on my own dime with my own kids. I'll buy myself a drink if I want one. We decide what we are going to do. We eat lunch on the cheap; whole-wheat bagels with peanut butter we brought from home. For dinner we go to a restaurant called "eat" (intentionally not capitalized). We are underdressed, but my kids are happy and well behaved, and I can pay for anything we order. We are seated outside, at a square table for four, in a parking lot patio surrounded by stringed lights. Zaki asks who will sit in the extra chair.

You can, I tell him. *You can be whoever you want while you're in it.*

He considers this for a moment. *I'll be Baba*, he decides. Even this testament to the brokenness of our family does not make me very sad. I record him making a deep voice and playing Karim and send it to Karim using my phone.

At the beach, the boys play in the surf and I read and take notes, pausing to peer up over the top of my book every paragraph or so. I spread the beach towel, a thin pink and orange striped rectangle of terrycloth bought in the hotel gift shop, directly beside the lifeguard's chair and instruct the children to stay near both him and me. The lifeguard is my quiet, watchful, un-demanding co-parent.

Zaki comes to me frequently, bringing fistfuls of wet sand. Sam comes only to deposit or retrieve his boogie board as he switches between swimming deep in the ocean and riding the waves. After a couple of hours, Sam tells me he will sit on the sand with Zaki if I want to take a swim.

Should I? I ask him.

Definitely, he replies. *It makes you feel like Nana.*

Like Nana is near? Or like Nana himself?

He bites his lip, thinking. *Both.*

The water is colder than is comfortable. I walk into it with purpose, bringing one foot in front of the other in wide circles, like a tightrope walker. Before long I have passed the point where the waves crash into foamy explosion. Now the water rolls smoothly in great green velvety humps. It feels as though I am moving through nearly set gelatin. I am alone; most people are not so far out. I get the sense that no one is watching me, and this frightens and frees me. The sky, overcast when we lay our blanket out, has brightened to a Mediterranean blue, with big, boiling white clouds in patches. I wonder what the sky was like the day my father drowned. I don't think I've ever gone this far into the ocean in my own company. I have always been with my father and later with my husband. This is brand new, and I feel strong.

Back at the hotel, after a greasy pizza dinner, the boys get in one double bed and I get in the other (before the night is over one or both will surely migrate to mine). I am reading, and they are squabbling. This hushed squabbling is their bedtime ritual. I don't encourage it, but there seems to be nothing I can do to stop it. Finally I look up. *What's the argument about tonight, boys?*

Sam says, *He's asking questions that make no sense. I just want to go to sleep.*

Well ask me, then, Z.

When the whole world breaks open, God will come out. Right, Mama?

Yes, I tell him. *I think that's right.*

Carrying

He is carrying me up from the car parked at the bottom of the hill while I pretend to be asleep. I dozed off watching the moon follow us through the window and when we stop I wake, but keep my eyes shut. He knows I am pretending, because I can't help giggling at his jokes. He squeezes my sides a little, jiggles the arm supporting me up and down. Laughs. *Eh! You're awake!* But he carries me anyway, up all the steps, because he is my father.

When he is gone and I remember this, it will seem unbelievable. That someone would carry me, knowing I don't really need it, wanting nothing in return.

Chicken Soup

A Wikipedia search on chicken soup makes no mention of Indian, or much less Bangladeshi, chicken soup traditions. Perhaps it is an oversight. Perhaps the fact that the soup is more of a "soupy chicken" than a chicken soup; served on a plate, over a bed of rice, precludes it from being included in a list of bowl-dwelling soups. This lightly-spiced chicken floating in pale gravy is a classic whose ingredients can be found in any American grocery store. The recipe is not exact—anything that travelled more than eight thousand miles in 1972 in the head of my mother, a sweet, docile new bride had to be flexible. You must have ginger and onions of course. And whole spices—sticks of cinnamon that curl in on themselves, pods of cardamom, peppercorns, and little rattle-shaped black cloves. Potatoes are nice, but not a requirement. They turn into lovely yielding pillows of softness, barely needing to be chewed before melting and sliding down your throat like a luxury. Be sure to have plenty of juicy lemons, cut into wedges to squeeze over your plate before you eat.

Are her limbs well rounded and her toenails painted? Is she comforting, a woman with large breasts and thick lips who smells like perfume? Does she dust her dresser twice a week?

The best way to cook it is with a whole chicken (or two), cut into eight pieces. I have the butcher remove the gnarliest pieces but my mother does not. In this respect, my mother is less delusional than I.

Is she delusional? Or is she matter-of-fact, scientific, and accepting of his flaws, of our marriage, of the fact that he has long been broken of the habit of trusting anyone?

It can be made with boneless chicken breasts cut into bite-sized cubes, colorless and featureless once cooked. Innocuous, unrecognizable, there's no need to confront what it is you have done, and to whom. This is the easy route, but if you choose it, the finished dish will lack the salty dimension marrow and blood release into the stew.

Eventually she will want a baby or two to bring to her breast, toddlers to zip into coats against the American winter. Will these little Bangla-speaking children eventually force my sons to the margins of their father's heart?

But I am getting ahead of myself, talking about cooking bones. There are steps to be completed long before this, when you've first returned home with a Styrofoam carton of chicken. You may have decided the fate of the chicken long before you set out for the butcher's shop, or it may have been spur-of-the-moment when faced with the butcher's questioning yes as you stepped up to the counter. You may have faltered, distracted by the lollipop he holds out to your preschool son, or by the put-together lady before you who ordered four little steaks for a perfect square family.

She is probably book-smart, easily amused, quiet, a movie-watcher. An accountant maybe, drunk after two rum-and-cokes. Not a whiskey drinker.

Someone may have told you that ginger does not need to be peeled before being ground. Tell my mother this and she may remain outwardly neutral about the vulgarity of that proposition while telling you evenly that it most certainly does. So peel it and then grate it by hand or blend it in your little mini-food processor. Be lazy and chop it roughly like I do, but the results won't be the same. The ginger will just sit atop the chicken, always a bit aloof, not quite integrated.

Or perhaps she will be more interested in my sons than I am. What I consider "little kids throwing a ball," she may find fascinating. She may know instinctively not to bring a book to the game; she may not even have the inclination. Perhaps it is I who will finally be pushed to the margins.

The vulnerable chicken, naked and bloody, must be smothered in plain yogurt mixed with the ginger and salt and pepper. Let this sit in a glass bowl on your countertop and turn your back to it. If you have other things to attend to, cover it and stick it in the refrigerator. Whenever you come back, it will be ready.

She must appreciate his body, the few scars on it attained in predictable ways—the round indentation on his shoulder from childhood immunization and calluses on his palms from hours at the gym. His smooth, muscled back cleared of hair by the trimmer wielded by one of the children and maybe one day—but not yet—her. She must run her toes along his calves and feel the weight of his hips between her soft thighs and feel lucky.

When you return to the kitchen, take a large round onion and peel it—you can't have heard anyone tell you that the papery skin has any destiny other than being discarded, so there's no need to ask my mother and risk her silent judgment (she has already judged you, though so subtly you'd never know it). Slice the onion thinly and try to keep the slices uniform. If your hands are unaccustomed to this work, don't worry—in this task, speed is prized above accuracy. While you're doing this, have some light colored oil heating in a pot. The pot you use is up to you. My mother prefers a stainless steel flat-bottomed wok, available at any shopping mall department store (never buy your pots in a set at a super-store—if you look, there are sales to be had on the good, name-brand stuff, clip the coupons when they come in the Sunday paper). I prefer a brightly colored enameled cast-iron dutch oven, which heats evenly and looks hip.

What does she think of the care he puts into dressing, into masking the thinning hair at the crown of his head? Does she find it a little egomaniacal, a little contrived? Or does she appreciate a man who loves himself as much as she loves him?

Heat the oil, and test it with a peppercorn. If bubbles form around it, give it company in the form of five more peppercorns, four cardamom pods, three of those darling cloves that remind you of a flower on a stem and two cinnamon sticks the length of your ring-finger. If like me you prefer your comfort food to stand up to you, add two whole dried red chili peppers to the pot as well. Let everything sizzle and darken a few shades, and then allow the onions to go in with a scream. By this I mean that the onions, or more precisely the water in them, will scream when they make contact with the oil. If it gives you some relief, you may choose to scream yourself. No one is listening.

Do they fight? Or is she too even-tempered to fight? Does she just sulk quietly and withdraw? Perhaps this is the best way, to wait until he asks after the grievances, pleads to hear what he has done wrong. And then maybe she tells him meekly that her feelings have been hurt and he envelops her in his arms and promises to do better next time.

Watch the onions, and stir them frequently with a wooden spoon. You don't want them to brown and grow crisp, to allow the heat to make its mark on them. You want them soft and pliable, yellow and translucent. Seeing them swim in the shallow oil, the heat and steam rising up to your face, you may feel like humming a peaceful, meaningless tune. Do this, because still, no one is listening.

Does she laugh easily, encourage him to lighten up? Or does she step back and allow him to brood while she goes about her business? Or do his dark periods tinge her days and weigh on her?

But don't get distracted. There are potatoes to peel. Don't even discuss this with my mother. You and I know, the peel contains nutrients—without it, potatoes are little more than white bread grown underground. The peel shows that the potatoes pushed out roots and staked a claim in the earth, that worms wound their way around those roots and someone on all fours burrowed to retrieve them. The peels are spotted and masculine, the white flesh is feminine, comforting. In this you have no choice: poke the eyes out with a knife, remove the peels quickly, feed the whole unsightly mess to the garbage disposal.

She was raised back home. Like him, like all of his friends, like my mother. Not an American like me. She would know better than to confront things directly, to talk back to his parents or her own. She would know how to get her way without getting dirty.

Chop the potatoes into quarters. They should be roughly the same size as the chicken pieces. If your onions are ready, put it all in the pot—chicken, potatoes, yogurt-ginger. Stir it once, turn the heat to low and put the lid on it. Even covered, the smells will waft through the house. Hang your coat in your closet and close your bedroom door. You don't want to smell like dinner everywhere you go. As it is, your hair will smell like fried onions until you shampoo it three times. Put up a pot of rice. If you don't know how to cook rice, maybe I've wasted my time by telling you all of this. Maybe you're even more American than me and you just won't understand.

Just Like Your Father

When I was ten I dressed as my father for Halloween. I wore an old pair of his glasses, a name badge from a conference he'd attended, carried his briefcase, wore one of his enormous suit coats.

In my twenties when my mother tells me I am just like my father, she means: unreliable, self-centered, not properly interested in staying still or being a parent. Or at least that's what I think she means.

As a child, when my father was traveling I would wear his kurta, sprayed with his cologne, to sleep. There's something particularly appealing about the absent. There is something noble about longing.

My mother was the winner of popularity contests. *Her* mother said she should have been a politician. My mother's father was a politician. The gravity of that sly insult, the passive, *You're just like your father* hangs in the air in the moment before my mother laughs. For my mother and her mother, the allegiance of their daughters required division from their fathers.

I will never have this conversation with her. She will deny it. Or worse, she will accept it, and all I will have accomplished is hurting her. Sliding this pain back across the table to her.

Now when my mother says, *You're like your father,* she means it as a compliment, but I can't take it as such, because my father was somebody better suited to being an uncle or a friend, not a reliable person, a person who could not be expected to do things he didn't want to do. He took pride in his children, who we became, what we accomplished, but took no part in the doing. As I sit in a coffee shop writing this, my children are attending soccer games and music practices with their father.

Mortality

I have written him out of stories because I am embarrassed. At how I treated him, at how little I regarded him. How right after he died all the spaces became rich with clues. Suddenly I wanted to know him. How did death surprise me?

Seeking

I am twelve years old. I have managed to work up the courage to ride my bicycle far away from the house, pedaling with scabbed knees down the street to the edge of the neighborhood. Beyond where the tame lawns and bushes encircle, as though in worship, the single old oak tree whose trunk is three times thicker than that of any of the other trees in the neighborhood. I drop my bicycle on its side and enter the path behind it on foot. I follow its curve into a less tame place, shaded and moist, smelling of clay and cold water slipping over black-green rocks. Here in this little bit of nature, in this sliver of almost wild I imagine myself ancient, I imagine myself useful.

But now I am a woman. I open my eyes and say to the girl: *You will always seek out these places, where the lawn is less manicured, where the earth doesn't hide her softness or her cunning. Here is a life of dappled light that cannot be paved over or repainted to conceal the inevitable seasons of harshness. In this place, of more dark than light, of uncertainty and chaos, you must learn to be.*

Living

The living room was his room. He had decorated it completely, ordering the furniture on a business trip to Indonesia without consulting my mother. He chose ornately carved claw and ball furniture—mirrors and coffee tables with crevices that required a cotton swab to properly dust. My mother chose sensible furniture for the rest of the house: Formica-topped tables and chairs that could be wiped clean, duvet covers so the comforters could be spared stains of tea.

Early in the morning sometimes I'd wake and find him sitting in his sleep-rumpled white kurta with the newspaper in one of the large chairs upholstered in bright tapestry in the living room. He always seemed to be an ample man, but at ten or eleven, I could squeeze into the chair beside him, his arm around me. His eyebrows are tangled, his face exposed, the large thick-framed glasses sit on the table, their hooked arms folded beneath them.

Sometimes he told me stories of a little boy and his sister. Always ending in, *And do you know who that little boy was? Me. And that was my big sister, Baji. She always loved me. She died too young.* I saw his eyes wet, but I do not remember tears spilling over the rim of his lower lids. I knew nothing of death, of loss, of what it costs to remember someone so they can continue to live.

Watching

My father's face was usually obscured by a camera clutched in his palm, pressed to the hollow around his eye. He saw the world as a photograph waiting to be taken, a film to capture and replay at will.

He recorded us eating and sleeping, mouths open. Slowly waking, getting into the car, walking down the street gossiping and arguing throwing tantrums and laughing.

We scowled at the camera, covered our faces, demanded he delete swaths of film, refused to watch the replay on the living room TV, delivered lectures on our rights to privacy, extracted oaths that he would never show them to anyone else.

When he died, we watched him leave the hotel, disappear through the glass doors, appear once more in the window as he passed.

He did not turn his gaze to the security camera perched high in the lobby. He did not know we would be watching.

Fathers Like Giants

Our fathers were way above us, higher than the clouds, taking care of things, taking care of our mothers, like giants who would catch us if we fell, though we did not notice them until they were gone. They took us to see things we didn't want to see, protected us from things we wanted to do.

Once, at a fair in Dhaka, a young man purposely bumped into my sister. My father, walking behind, bumped into him with the girth of his belly, sending him askew and when their eyes met, my father said, *I thought you liked bumping into people.*

And just as we had forgotten he was there walking behind us, we sometimes forget now that he is not.

Utah

The ragged, voluptuous lines of mountains are the silhouettes of giant, slumbering women.

When I get into the bathtub I am reminded of this.

I feel like a giant myself, in so small a container. I see my belly quiver beneath the clear hot water and it seems to me that I am not controlling this quiver. It exists separately from me. I am not this body any more than I am one of those giant slumbering women who sit along the skyline, one bending a knee, one resting her hand on another's hip.

And one day this body will be placed in a container not much bigger than the bathtub and this landscape of flesh will again belong to no one.

Crying

The best way to cry is in the arms of a lover, but lovers grow tense when you cry in their arms. They feel powerless, they feel responsible and impotent.

They think they are supposed to ask what's wrong and offer solutions.

They do not understand that I do not want to be interrupted, that there is nothing they can do. That I would never give anyone alive the power to be the cause of my tears, or the solution.

Sacrifice

Bakr-eid is the Muslim festival celebrating Isaac's heroic willingness to sacrifice his son on the altar of God, and God's offering up of a ram at the last moment. In Dhaka, the occasion is celebrated with the slaughtering of cows and goats citywide. The animals are brought from the countryside and tethered in carports. They chew hay and stare blankly when the city children pet them. On the morning of Bakr-Eid, their throats are cut in God's name and the blood flows down driveways and into gutters. By afternoon, all that is left are piles of fur and bone by the sides of the roads. When I was sixteen, I was in Dhaka for Bakr-Eid. I began to worry when the animals arrived in the city and my cousins began to argue over which of them would get to perform the slaughter. My father, seizing the opportunity to do something grand and ridiculous, took me to stay in a western hotel where all of the grit and ritual of Bangladeshi culture was distilled into hand-embroidered items in the gift shop. We stayed there from the night before until the afternoon, leaving the hotel to join family celebrations, my eyes closed the entire car ride.

My father cannot shield me from this. I have flown these thousands of miles to offer myself and my own son up for this task.

We are at the airport. Sam has a brand new passport. On the application for an expedited passport they want to know what the hurry is. In block letters I write: DEATH IN THE FAMILY. Zaki will stay with Karim. Earlier in the day we went to Zaki's class play, a kindergarten production of *The Rainbow Fish*, after which other parents were thanked for sewing costumes, making the program, doing the make-up. For Sam's elementary school play the year before I had sewn thirty kimonos for a Japanese-influenced Shakespeare performance. I am no longer that mother.

I am not sure if I remembered to pack underwear. I know I've packed shorts and T-shirts for Sam, mosquito spray and nail polish from the drugstore. I'm not sure why I bought so much nail polish. I will wear my mother's or my cousin's or my aunt's clothes. My phone rings again and again. My cousins tell me to be strong, be safe, to let them know when I've reached. They tell me that the first group of travelers—my aunt and sisters and nieces—has already reached and will be there to receive us. While we wait to board the plane, I buy Sam ice cream.

On an airplane it is hard to hear anything other than your own thoughts over the engine. The captain, who we never see, switches the seatbelt light on and off. Sam watches a movie, plays the video games attached to the monitor on the seatback in front of him. I think about swimming with my father. I think about all the things I've left undone.

My sisters are waiting at the airport when we arrive. They are usually disconnected by their personality differences, by a sibling rivalry that grew into a deep cleft of mistrust. In grief, though, they are a pair. We climb into the backseat of my grandmother's car, all four of us, Sam's backpack in the passenger seat beside the driver. We have no father now, never had brothers. Sam, eleven years old and sitting on my sister's lap, is the oldest blood-related man in our immediate family.

My parents left their apartment tidy, but they were very much in the middle of living. Their nightclothes hang on hooks in their bathroom; my father's extra pair of glasses remains on his nightstand. We wonder if we should make it look less normal for my mother, who has not yet arrived with the body, but do not know what she needs.

We bury our dead immediately—by the next prayer time. Ostensibly to limit a prolonged deification of the dead, of body worshipping, the collecting of relics—locks of hair, bits of fingernails. But really, because it's hot, and everyone should be spared the visual of the disintegration of their loved ones. We were not.

The wooden crate holding my father's body was put into an air-conditioned van. We were promised a refrigerated truck, but that may have been a translation problem. At any rate, the van broke down three minutes out of the airport gate, and the rough box had to be moved to a passing two-wheeled wagon pulled by a few men. My parents' apartment wasn't far from the airport, and our cars followed behind the wagon in the morning heat. They unloaded the crate in the garage of the building and somebody paid the men and there we were. How so many people had gathered in the time it had taken us to collect our parents from the airport, I didn't know, but there were throngs in the shade of the garage and chairs had been set up and cars had been removed.

And we were facing the crate and somebody had a crowbar and we turned the kids—Sam eleven and Inshira thirteen and Jenna nine to face the other direction, shielding them, allowing the crowd to press in. And when the men with the crowbars heaved and split and pried the lid of the box containing my father off, we gasped and in that weakness, we made cracks in the human barricade and the kids turned and the smell of an old refrigerator being opened—of dry ice and formaldehyde—came out. It was the chemical smell of a sealed space. Sam gasped and said *that's not my grandfather* and ran up the stairs, ran all the way to the fifth floor and my mother kneeled there beside the casket and I sat next to her, staring at this flattened nose plugged with cotton and the darkened skin—he would have hated to be seen so darkened—and his head wrapped in gauze and where were his hands I wanted to see his hands. His eyebrows were waxed and triangular—really the only thing I could recognize of my father was his eyebrows. His skin was sort of flaking and the flies came quickly and dead bodies are supposed to be cold, but when my mother made me kiss him—she begged me to, because in Islam a marriage ends at death and so she couldn't kiss him though she wanted to. And I couldn't refuse, I had already made so many mistakes as a daughter how could I refuse her this, I tasted formaldehyde and attar and his skin was warm and giving way beneath my lips and his lips were so darkened and she kept asking me, *Doesn't he look good? Doesn't he look so peaceful?*

And I had already failed and so I told her yes and fanned the flies and waited for the right moment to ask her to let him go.

Conversation

Part of you is always alone, you can't help it. A good part of you is you, yourself. But again, there are people. You have to make a compromise between that aloneness and this crowd.
—Naushaba Khatoon (my grandmother)
December 2010

In Dhaka, Bangladesh, one is never alone. An operatic melody exists in the unremitting voices heard from sun up until late night throughout the city. Long vowels joined by soft consonants—hawking, greeting, gossiping. The recorded political tirades looped over loudspeakers and played from scooters buzzing around the city drone in angry, repetitive bass tones. There is percussion: the pounding hammers of construction, the punctuation of car horns, the sharp trill of rickshaw bells: two bursts in quick succession. Five times throughout the day, rounds of azan, the call to prayer, are sung from more than a thousand weather and pollution beaten domed minarets around the city. The words are identical, but each starts at a slightly different moment. The sounds of the azan are unlike the city's other voices—harsh Arabic consonants, an affected nasality—a Middle Eastern chorus to the city's distinctly Bangla song.

My grandparents' apartment in Dhaka is just as it always was: plastic tablecloths, wicker bookshelves packed with dusty Bangla and English books. The living room still adheres to a black and white color scheme and my grandparents' bedroom is strictly shades of blue. The walls are laden with photographs and paintings of two men: my grandfather, round-faced, smooth-shaven, balding, bespectacled, and the Bengali poet Rabindranath Tagore, long-faced with sunken eyes and a pointed beard.

My grandparents are careful, speck-less. They wear starched white and gray clothing; no hair stands out of place. Even beset with dementia, my grandfather's face is carefully shaved by his nurse at the breakfast table each morning, the shaving cream applied with a broad brown-handled brush. My grandmother's large bifocal glasses stay on her face from morning until night, magnifying her large eyes and the upraised moles around them. She keeps a heavy bunch of keys in the waistband of her sari, then the pocket of her nightgown. At night she sleeps with the keys under her pillow.

My grandfather hums to himself and asks the same questions again and again. He points to a large portrait of himself and says, *That is my father. He was a great man, a General.*

My grandfather's father was, according to my grandmother, a ne'er-do-well. A member of a prominent religious family in his village, he traded amulets and prayer beads for free meals and cash. My grandfather, an atheist, never thought much of him (or Generals) before. Though his dementia has been steadily invading for five years now, there is a part of me that doesn't believe it. There is a flash in his eye, a curve of his lip that makes me feel like perhaps he is faking it.

My grandmother assures me he isn't. *It is so lonely*, she says. *There he is, there sits my friend. But where is the conversation? It is just me, alone. And he, a body.*

Holes

Visit after visit, I watched my grandfather grow smaller, quieter, more confused, shrinking out of sight. I can tell you how the skin on his face smelled, I can tell you about the rough brownness of it. I can tell you about how he hummed while shuffling around the apartment, how I would recognize his voice anywhere. I can tell you that by the time I was supposed to be mourning his death, I did not have any capacity for mourning left. There were too many holes in my world already. I couldn't think about one more, one that had started to open so many years before. I can tell you that one day I know I will mourn him, and mourn my failure to give my grandmother the satisfaction and pleasure of seeing me grieve for him.

Circles

My mother and I are lying in bed, arms folded over our eyes to block the light in her dim apartment because she never opens the blinds, because natural light irritates her. She turns on lamps to read and then shields her eyes to nap.

I don't say this as an assault against my mother—it is just the sort of thing that I find most charming about her. The odd circles she runs in to make herself comfortable.

She tells me, *In 1971, your sister was a baby in my arms and someone threw a brick at the windshield of the car and your father had to drive home so slowly to keep the glass from shattering and falling all over us and when we made it he said, "We can't live in a place like this," so we came to America.*

I ask why I have never heard this. Why has the story always been that he was looking for opportunity and was tired of living with bad memories or was restless? Why wasn't this our narrative? This makes for another history altogether.

She says, *What difference does it make? We are here.*

six things that broke my heart this week

1. My mother's loss of faith in me
2. Zaki says he doesn't get to kiss me enough
3. The sound of the ocean
4. Pediatric cancer patients
5. The memory of my father's hand around mine
6. Loneliness

Calling

There are days when the memory of my father—his Old Spice cologne, his striped light and dark blue sweater, the way he pointed with his middle finger, thumped me too hard on the back when he was excited to see me—arrives so clearly, I cannot breathe.

There are days when grief arrives, digs its chin into my shoulder, presses its hand to the small of my back, and reminds me that even if I don't acknowledge it, even if I can resist turning to embrace it, it will wait.

It will call my name in my father's voice, just before I fall asleep.

Tell Me Yourself

I cannot believe my father is dead. Until I have this dream, months after he is buried:

I am watching TV and a gray cordless phone on the coffee table keeps interrupting. I try to answer it, but there is no one on the other end. My father appears. *My friend keeps trying to call and you keep hanging up on him.*

I don't look at him, I just say, *No, I'm trying answer it.* And keep changing channels.

Let it ring for longer, beta. We need to buy a new phone, when I get back to Dhaka I'll see what my cousin has and get that.

I am annoyed. Even though we can no longer ask Karim about what phone is best, I am capable of finding my parents a phone that works.

My mother appears across the room, a travel bag open on the arm of a sofa. She says, *Abba is going to go there and there and there over the next couple of weeks, finishing off this thing and the other that he's left. I am trying to pack this bag for him, but I don't know what to put in it.*

Why does he have to go? I ask

And she lets go of the bag and looks at me with weary eyes and says, *Won't he want to use his visa one more time?*

And I say, *Wait I don't understand, is he alive?*

And she looks at me and looks away, so I turn to where he is standing in the corner, in his blue striped sweater with a navy suit jacket over it and I get up and run to him. Put my arms around him. He is taller than I remembered. Or I am smaller.

Abba, Abba, look at me. Tell me. Are you alive or are you dead? And he looks down and I see his face, his face from when I was a child, smooth shaven and black haired in the black glasses with lenses tinted dark as though he'd just been in the sun, and I rest my head on the crest of his belly and he puts his arms around me and kisses my head and I know.

Faith

After he died, my sister or my mother or my aunt or someone said, *he's got one grandchild with him. He's probably in heaven with the baby and his own parents.*

What a gift faith is. Of the teachings from my Islamic upbringing I believe this, most of all, to be true: *There are people whose eyes and ears are closed, those who cannot believe. Have mercy on them, for they will suffer.*

Not believing, not feeling any sense of certainty about the afterlife, is suffering.

There is a childlike innocence in those with deep faith. The sweet, sweet conviction of feeling like they know beyond any doubt what the meaning of life is, what is right and what is wrong. Why don't I have this?

All I Can Give

He's a teenager now, and his fears and grief show up only as anger. Usually directed at me. He slams doors and mopes and tells me I'm a terrible mother. Glares at me with tears suspended in the web of his long, thick eyelashes. Tells me he wishes he was at his father's house, tells me he wishes he lived only with his father. I am not perfect; I am not patient. I try to hug him, he shrugs away. I try to ignore him and he slams cabinet doors, hits ping-pong balls off the dining table until they ricochet off the ceiling and the artwork on the walls. I tell him to calm the fuck down and quit being a dick. This makes him angrier, more certain of how unfit I am as a mother.

I am not nice, but I am the nicer parent. I am the nicer parent, but he misses his father, who is in Dhaka, sitting in a hospital room I will not see, while *his* father is forced alive by a ventilator that expands and contracts his lungs with a hiss and then a release, pushing oxygen through a tube into his prone body. I can imagine this man I used to love suffering through it. I am relieved that I no longer love him, that his grief is no longer my concern.

But I know that each loss brings up previous losses, that each bout of grief awakens dormant sadness. And I hold my breath, brace myself to absorb the impact because the grief of my children will always be mine.

All I can do is take them for a hike. It is autumn, and the trail is thick with fallen leaves concealing the hazards of loose rocks and jutting tree limbs.

All I can give them, when I am charged with helping them understand things I cannot understand, is proof that the world goes on.

All I can give them is a river that cuts Maryland from Virginia and stones to throw into it.

All I can give them, when the river is low, is the noble vulnerability of exposed tree roots.

All I can give them, when the water level rises, is the wonder of looking at the places we once stood. Places temporarily submerged.

Ash

The best thing about being in my thirties:
I am young enough to fall in love all the time,
and old enough to feel relieved when it's over.

Apples

I.

The apple
doesn't fall
it glistens
when ripe
it is plucked
wrenched
from the tree
and then
blamed for being a temptation.

II.

I want to be dead woman flawless. Legendary,
two dimensional. Like my grandmother,
the gold standard of Bengali beauty impressed
through photo frame glass upon my childhood:
pale skin, thick hair, narrow nose, big eyes.
Each night, one hundred tugs on my nose to make it long
by the dark, broad-nosed woman who cared for me.
She wanted me to be prettier. Now I want to be prettier
than your girlfriend, prettier than your wife

I want mine to be the face you risk your neck reaching for,
the apple you cannot resist twisting from the tree.

III.

When yet another man knocks
smelling of salt and cloth
demanding a piece of you,
Take the knife from his hand.
choose the piece of your flesh
to surrender. Carve it out cleanly,
put it in his palm, smile sweetly.
You may be tempted
to brandish the blade in his direction.
Let him go unscathed
keep slicing
for each of their hungry mouths
until all that remains is your frame
shut the door and take stock.

This is what you have to give.

Mud

Even before I was sure I would leave Karim, Nick began to offer love. He was the one who showed me I was fire, that I could jump from the ring of stones containing me. I consumed him like a trail of dried leaves as I went. Together we gasped for air, heads thrown back, loose parts jiggling, in laughter and in tears. With him I felt happy, enough, tethered. I wanted to drink it down, continue to be selfish, to take what I did not deserve. To use the magic that came into my brain from sleeping next to him, to exploit the confidence that came from having his unwavering, unconditional love.

But my children needed me to go slowly into these muddy waters. I have claimed myself from the pyre, in doing so have split them in half, left their eyelashes singed, their cheeks and ribs smudged with ash. The smell of smoke will always remind them of childhood. What more can I ask of them?

The Whole Truth

I couldn't stay with him because I didn't want my kids to have to suffer from me being in a new relationship.

I'm sorry. That's not the whole truth about Nick. A mother sacrificing great love to give herself to her children. That's admirable, selfless. Who could blame me? But that's not how it happened, just how it turned out.

I couldn't stay with Nick because I didn't want to. I couldn't give myself over to him. Couldn't be faithful, couldn't compromise, couldn't see him as enough. Couldn't forgive his imperfections, though he forgave mine.

Karim would tell you, as he told me from the start, that Nick was just a rebound. An elastic impulse, nothing serious, a delusion.

I think Nick would tell you, (if he talks to you, he doesn't talk to me anymore) that we needed each other for a time. That he waited for me to realize that we could be happy together. That one day he met someone who looked at him the way he looked at me and he stopped waiting.

When I saw myself through his eyes, I saw someone I liked. That's who I fell in love with. Myself, in his eyes.

That's who I keep falling in love with. Myself, in all of their eyes. And when I don't like what I see, I find another pair of eyes.

History

I have been considering love since my very first crush, on a boy named Douglas in my third grade class. He was the class clown. He wore tie-dye T-shirts, so I got a tie-dye backpack. I don't think he ever acknowledged me. There was a boy in aftercare with me, Nathaniel, who sat in the swing beside me on the playground and such—but I wasn't interested. Douglas was an *idea*. His mother baked pies, he lived on the farm that our class took a fieldtrip to in the Fall. He was blonde and freckled, he fit in. He was the exact opposite of me. Even then, before I had experienced romantic love, there was an instinctive arching towards longing.

That was the same year I moved from a diverse, secular, Montessori school to an almost exclusively white, traditional school. It was the same year that my nanny, who had slept in my bedroom with me since I was ten months old, left in the middle of the night without saying goodbye. It was the year I began to sleepwalk. This may be coincidence. But I can't help but see the parallels as I've returned to using love and longing as a diversion from the actual demands of my life, a make-believe world where I by turn have no control and all the control, where the outcome is of little consequence. I cannot blame all of my brokenness on Karim—he has taught me new cause for caution, certainly, but my love for longing existed before I met him.

Danger

Even in cultures where it is not considered necessary in the arrangement of a marriage, love's power is acknowledged. The reason boys and girls are kept separate is because love can strike anywhere there is space. People in love cannot be trusted to make decisions for themselves or their families. It is dark magic, opium haze, that thing that you wake from, disoriented, body aching. Love is dangerous, addictive, something I serve myself in small doses to soften reality.

Boston

I fell in love for a night with a man on a snowy sidewalk in Boston. We never went on a date, never ended up in a hotel room, no long stretch of time alone together. We had drinks with friends and something between us glowed. Sometimes I think of his smile or the way he kissed the top of my head before I got into a cab and said, *You are fucking lovely.*

This little moth of love, suspended in amber, no future, no complication. No chance for him to learn that I'm not that lovely after all.

Fleeting

When our eyes meet across the room it is as though a bubble has floated in through a window I hadn't meant to leave ajar. It lands on my palm

                    quivering

familiar and unexpected: no less real for its fragility, no less iridescent for its impracticality.

Shores

Love is a feral force which uncovers a wild streak in each of us. It seems the wilder a person, the more intense the passion they inspire. The adrenaline rush of uncertainty, of highs and lows, of anguish-filled wondering does not exist within a healthy love affair, one in which connection between partners is a solid fact, intentions are clear. The thrill gives way to a desire for domestication and possession, for a mutual taming. While we love the sheer power of our wildness, it terrifies us. We swim in these waters, but as we are submerged, we dream of the shore.

Safe

Karim is right. I'm a mess. I don't know how to be a grown up; my car insurance lapses every few months. Not because I haven't set aside the money, but because I don't open the envelopes when the bills arrive. I pile them on my desk and forget about them. The weeks pass. There's no milk in the fridge, and the kids aren't coming home for days so I drink my coffee black and on my way home from work I buy a box of wine and a cup of noodles for dinner, and never make it to the cup of noodles before falling asleep, glass of wine on my bedside table (which is a metal filing cabinet with a plank of wood over the top, piled high with books I haven't finished reading).

After every romance ends, there is a part of me that worries maybe he was right. Maybe I'm not meant to do this, not meant to be in a relationship with anyone, not grateful enough for love given.

After every romance ends, I hear his words in my ears, the last time he got really angry with me, while we were discussing child support on the phone when I stood safe and alone at the wooden table in my apartment across town.

Somebody is going to knock you down, Seema. And I hope they kill you.

Risk

When he enters, he takes off his shoes, places his gun on a chair at my dining table.

We eat dinner, sit on the couch. He flexes his arm, places my hand on his bicep.

This show of his strength is a flirtation, the feather-fanning dance of every courtship I've had since I was thirteen.

Gently, he runs his fingers along the length of my forearm, encircles my wrist between his thumb and middle finger, barely touching my skin.

His eyes are kind, his face a smiling moon, his lips on mine are tender, yielding, respectful. His laughter comes easily.

The fragility of my body is a fact. I am assessing the risk of entering a fight I will not win, a grip I won't escape without surrendering a limb. Just under the surface of my smile, I am making a plan, deciding what I will leave behind when I have to run.

Suffering

Lifelong romantic partnership makes perfect sense with respect to division of labor, finances, emotional security, child-rearing. Commitment is the best thing for living a peaceful life. What makes absolutely no sense is passion, which thrives on instability and conflict. And yet, that is what I crave, when the facts of the world become too bleak, I seek a less serious suffering. Perhaps nothing makes us feel more alive than suffering. Unrequited love, a journey traversed largely in the mind, which leaves us hungry, can satisfy this thirst.

Obsession

For the past few weeks, I have been obsessed with Damian Rake, a man I met through work, who was nothing but polite. It didn't occur to me to be obsessed with him until he befriended me on Facebook and started to send me text messages—all *very* professional. Maybe a little friendly but by no means flirtatious. He's probably married. He doesn't know I'm alive—in the teen dream sense. He lives in Florida—*lives* in Florida. When he sends me an email or a text message or a package (yes, he once sent me a package) with a professionally friendly handwritten note, I squeal and take a picture of it and text it to Mark, a self-professed bear who also has a crush on Damian, but I claimed him first, so by the laws of sixth grade, he is my boyfriend. He is the boy I like who might even like me. One *really* has to read between the lines of the text messages to believe that—but I have spent the time and I am reasonably convinced.

About a month before I met him, I decided to stop dating stupid people. Six weeks before that, I had decided to date ONLY people who couldn't possibly engage me in heavy conversations or expect any real commitment from me—people so fucked up that I wouldn't ever be tempted to give in to relationship pressure and open a joint checking account. So I dated a local children's entertainer with a gambling addiction for a while, and got some good stories out of it—there was a convention he took me to afterhours where all children's entertainers were body painting one another and making lewd balloon animals and once he had a seizure during a performance and I swear to God I mimed on stage. But very soon he asked whether we had any orange juice and I thought, "For *us* to have orange juice, I'd have to have orange juice in my fridge and *you'd* have to have orange juice in the fridge at your house." And I knew it was probably time to extricate myself from the situation.

So my obsession with Damian is the next logical step. He is an artist (sigh) and manages a budget (sigh). He has no romantic interest in me—which has never been my type. I have always liked best the man who likes *me* best. I married the man who was the most obsessed with *me*—punching-windshields-out-of-jealousy obsessed—and since separating have found myself in relationships with one ego boost after the other. They love my work, they think I'm so clever, they can barely contain their glee when they introduce me to their friends. Damian takes twenty-four hours to reply to a text message, and I am obsessed.

Like Water

He stopped texting me back. Well, he cancelled dinner plans at the last minute so I broke up with him via text. Then he called me and asked for another chance. It's a long story, honestly, but the point is I broke up with him in words; he said he didn't want us to stop seeing each other. And then he disappeared.

I liked him. There were some weird things, sure. Like he had this extremist tattoo on his left pectoral. But he assured me it was from long ago. And he was a Scorpio, like Karim, which kind of bothered me. Is this too much identifying information? Whatever. He doesn't text, I'm sure he won't buy my book.

His mouth always tasted like water and I liked sleeping next to him.

Kingdom

Even requited love is a solitary pursuit. The object of our love, whoever he or she may be, is of no particular importance. The quickened heart, the challenge of deciphering signals, is no different whether the person upon whom we shine the full sun of our attention is extraordinary or average. What matters is that the feelings they elicit in us reflect how we want to feel. Love is the kingdom in which we allow ourselves the freedom to choose the unreasonable, and are rewarded for it by a surreal peak experience. Couples act against society, convention, parents, and common sense, and in exchange they are given access to an entire universe of two.

The exquisite thrill of gambling with something so real and intangible as one's own heart or the heart of another is no small part of the pleasure.

Ponies

She put her nose to my neck and said, *You smell like child-hood. You smell like My Little Ponies.* I could not afford not to follow this story, Nick. I am a writer. I have an interesting life, but I can write only so much about domestic abuse and war. I'm sorry that I hurt you.

Rebecca Solnit says, *Never turn down an adventure without a really good reason.* I'm sorry that you were not a good enough reason. If it makes you feel better, no other man ever has been either. No one loved me like you did. Even that was not reason enough.

Prey

Sometimes I feel as if I am curled into the depression of a teaspoon, knees to nose on worn cold metal. Halfway between the bowl I came from and the mouth that hungers for me.

Friends

For the third time, we fill our plastic cups. Our drink to-night is vodka and Mountain Dew. We decide to walk through the dark, warm night to the fountain just outside of the Base Commander's office window in the center of the Army post. Stone penguins squirt water from tubes in their mouths into the top tier, a large, scalloped concrete saucer steadily overflowing into the three-foot depth of the lower level, which is set into the ground. Steps lead down from street level to the grass encirclement. We walk up to the edge, slip off our shoes, dip our feet and legs in. Marcus warns me that if anyone comes, he will take off and leave me here. He could get fired, or be dropped in rank for this. He says he will take off his clothes as he runs.

They'll be looking for a Hispanic male in a blue polo shirt and khaki shorts. I'll be in my boxers.

You don't think running around base in your underwear will impact your career? I kick my feet back and forth, push-ing against the weight of the cool water. *If anyone comes, I'm going to say I'm a mental patient.*

We sit on the concrete lip at the fountain's edge, trad-ing anecdotes about places we've been, trouble we've gotten into. I can't remember what I'm wearing or what I look like today, don't care that I am smudged with paint and must smell like a full day of work. I am high on feeling loved for being funny and smart, for being un-intimidated and quick with a comeback—a girl that doesn't get offended easily; can check out other girls with the guys. A girl who's not really a girl. I haven't felt this way since I was in high school. Back then I was hindered by orthodontia and unease with my body, perpetually labeled friend material. Back then, I wanted more. Now it seems that men circle me hungrily, and all I want are people to laugh with.

And then he turns to me and leans back on his hands. Asks me what I want from him. I remember that I am no longer a girl.

Falling

I am afraid. Of falling. Anyone who offers to catch me I hate and anyone who makes no promises I love because the man who doesn't promise anything is the only honest man. And he will break my heart and I will wonder what I did wrong. I will wonder how he sleeps at night because leaving me was the stupidest thing he could have done. But I will know that if he had stayed, I would have left him.

Because what kind of idiot would want to be with me?

To Get Over Him

When the good memories perch on your shoulders, wring their pretty necks.

Plant the annoyances, the worst fights like seeds in the pit of your stomach. Before he is completely gone, allow them to grow into vines you can cling to.

On the day his mouth tastes like sour sadness and his presence feels like a cobra coiled around you, join your body with his one last time.

Then never do it again.

You Want Another Chance

Come, climb this mountain again. I have been waiting.

Arrive with your tools: lingering look, compliments in my language, cologne on your wrists and collarbone.

Be warned: this landscape is changed.

Rain washed away trails you carved, I have embedded a razor in every soft mound of clay that held the mark of your grip. Every foothold has been polished smooth. Trees you scarred to trace your path have near healed. There is nothing familiar here.

Choices

If, when he comes to me with head tilted, waiting, lingering in my sight line, I extend my hand, he will take it. He will step over the threshold with exaggerated reluctance and an approximation of tenderness. He will set me on fire and watch me burn. The embers will glow, my ashes will smother them.

What I Tell Them

Between bites of dessert and sips of wine, kisses and bouts of laughter, I tell them: *I am best in small doses. Enjoy my company, then leave me be.*

More laughter, a slow smile, raised eyebrow. Entranced, they reach for my hands, tell me not to worry about their hearts, promise to ask, to expect, nothing of me, ever.

I'm serious. There is no us. Here is me, there is you.

But when the sadness comes and loneliness blows against my skin, I fear they heed my warning.

Meeting

There is a visiting writer scheduled to visit the hospital. I have been planning his visit for months. The patients have read some of his stories, are looking forward to this opportunity. Some have even bought their own copies of his book. I was informed, as I was leaving the end-of-the-year elementary school parent social, that the class play was scheduled for the same day as his visit. A few of the mothers were leaning over the granite-topped island in the gleaming kitchen, becoming wine-affectionate with one another. I came in to say goodbye. *Thank you so much. I'll see you next week. Is the play at 5:30 or 6?* There is an exchanged glance (I may have imagined this).

The play is at 2:30, Alisha Stoneman tells me, eyebrows raised. That was definitely not imagined.

There had been about thirty minutes of conversation over white wine about how best to simulate a boulder on stage, about whether fake blood would traumatize the children. The husband and wife parent team that sews the costumes for nearly every school play (they are adorable) has been discussing their plans. They both work. They both have important high-profile jobs. I'm the asshole who didn't know when the class play was.

Which means I will have to make a choice: class play or veterans. This is how my choices always unfold: birthday party or veterans. Sick day or veterans. Rollerblading, swimming pool, elaborate home-cooked dinner or veterans. I make a plan to have it all: I will leave early, see him through the workshop with the patients who are in the partial hospitalization program, the session I have to be there for, and have a colleague cover the other writing workshop which is open to the entire hospital, including staff.

He is generous and honest with the group of twelve or so service members in the workshop I attend. Each of them writes about their military experience, even those who are openly angry whenever they are assigned to my writing group. Each wants to share their work. The group is supposed to end at 1:50. I planned to run to my car at 1:55 and make it to the play, which starts at 2:30. It is 2 and they are still reading and waiting for the writer's comments, which he offers slowly and thoughtfully. I can't leave before I've asked them to applaud and thank him, before I remind them to take their work, if it stirred something that will not settle, to their respective mental health providers. I jiggle my leg impatiently, clench my hands and then relax them, remind myself that my job is to maintain calm in the room. When finally we close, it is 2:05. I thank the writer, shake his hand with both of mine and run to my car. It is summer, and an afternoon storm has begun, my drive is delayed by a downpour that limits visibility. I enter the church basement just as the final applause has broken out.

I stand in the back soaking wet, a halo of frizz forming around my head, and join the clapping. Other parents turn to look at me sideways, sympathetic and judgmental. Glad they are not me. My plastic hospital badge is still clipped to the collar of my dress.

In the third row, Sam is sitting with his father and a woman I recognize (from light social media research with my cousins) as Karim's girlfriend, who lives with my children half the time, in the house I raised them in and left behind two years ago. Who I have not yet met. Her hair is straight and brushed and dry. She is carrying a Burberry bag and looks more like the other private school mothers than I do. One of the teachers, who just last week began reading my blog and sent me an email saying she is proud to know me, that Zaki brags about me, leads me to the makeshift backstage, puts her hands on my shoulders, and tells me that Zaki only had three lines, the play was short, that she is so sorry.

You're better than this, Seema, she tells me while I cry. I wipe my tears, thank her, and face the room of parents milling about.

Zaki is showing Karim and the girlfriend his school-work, which is laid out on a table for parents to peruse. Karim is dressed in a blue button down shirt tucked into salmon colored trousers. He is wearing yellow alligator loafers. He glances at me briefly when I approach. He has new glasses that do not suit him. This is a small gift.

Hi, I'm Seema, I say, reaching forward to shake her hand. *We haven't met. I'm Sam and Zaki's mother.* This comes out harsher and more pointed than I meant it to, the emphasis on mother sounds jealous and territorial.

Her smile is nervous. *Yes, I've heard so much about you. Nice to meet you.*

I turn away to make small talk with some of the other mothers. Alisha Stoneman is serving punch. What I need in this room are established allies. What I really want to do is hang out with kids. When I've made some loose prom-ises to *definitely get the kids together sometime over the summer*, I go play with the kids, who are high from the combination of unsupervised cupcake eating and post-performance ex-hilaration. We are having a dance party on the part of the blue-tiled floor that had been used as the stage. After a few minutes, a teacher comes over to tell the kids to calm down. *I don't know why you think this is a way to behave indoors*, she tells them sternly without looking directly at me. *You should know better than this.* I want to flick her off as she stomps away. I shrug at the kids, who roll their eyes and giggle.

It is Tuesday, so the boys will be going home with Karim. He and Sam come to where I'm standing and the crowd of children disperses. The girlfriend is sitting in a chair looking at Zaki's new yearbook, which I purchased, and so should be going home with. The order form came to both of us. If Karim wanted a copy for his house he should have ordered one. This is petty, so I turn to Sam and ask him to just make sure the yearbook makes it back to our house. This infuriates Karim. *Just because you're standing on a stage doesn't mean you have to be so dramatic.* He walks over and snatches the yearbook out of the girlfriend's hands and pushes it at me. He turns on his alligator heel and walks toward the door. The boys give me quick hugs and the girlfriend offers her hand. *It was nice to meet you*, she says before quickly following after him.

She has such nice manners. Where is her mother? Shouldn't someone warn her? That night in a lover's bed, the heat of his body wrapped around mine disrupts my sleep and her face rises again and again.

Safety Brief

Drive your own car, plan an escape route. Never come to a complete stop, keep moving. Know where your safe haven is.

Brace when he shows you muscles, the size of his hands, displays his strength.

Pay your own way, be on alert for:

exasperation, raised voice, balled fists, signs of temper

Your instincts are no good (but heed your fears). You cannot be trusted to make decisions. You aren't loved by everyone.

Be alert. Be wary of new friends. A wedding band means someone is texting you, will alert the authorities if you don't make it home.

You are safest alone. Pretending not to be.

Goldfish

With absolute conviction, you tell me what I should do about taxes or laws or finances—things I choose not to know, things I think you're smarter than me about. Your voice is assured as it turns to deep, low, chocolate monotone. I have doubts—something doesn't quite make sense. But I can't possibly know better than *you*.

So I try to swallow it whole.

It goes down like a goldfish: slippery, flopping, leaving scales on my tongue, threads of tail fins caught between my teeth. It lands in my stomach and flutters.

And when I discover I was right, I realize I have committed the worst sin. I have been disloyal to myself.

Flags

You explain that beauty invites conquerors desiring the thrust of flag into flesh.

This zeal is excessive. My center is liquid, molten beneath an easily shattered crust. I do not know how to protect my soft parts armed with only this fragile lattice of bone.

Bewitched

I gave you a red toothbrush after we fell asleep on the sofa watching a Japanese remake of that show where a witch marries a mortal and becomes a housewife. In the Japanese version the special effects are different, but the conflict is the same: a woman apologizing for her power, a man tolerating her in spite of it.

Driving

"My wife," he says, "is not like you. She isn't smart or courageous or driven. A person needs that."

His flattery is aimed at the newest version of me, hurtling down an unfamiliar highway in a rented car. I have spent five days at a professional conference wearing heels and dry clean only dresses. This man sits in the passenger seat next to me, blankly handsome, tall and broad. He wears jeans with a collared shirt and blazer and has had too much wine. In the back seat are our dinner companions, lively laughing women in their late twenties. We all met here in San Francisco at the conference.

I am pleased by his flattery in the way that all flattery pleases—this I cannot help. I imagine my ex-husband sitting next to some woman in a professional setting somewhere while *I* stayed home in a ponytail waiting for him to come home and throw his socks in the direction of the laundry and compliment me, make me feel strong and beautiful, make my small, domestic work seem important.

If this were my cartoon, I would open the passenger door and give him a push. He would fall woodenly out, sideways, knees still bent in sitting position and I would drive on satisfied, my hair blowing in the wind. If this were his movie, I would touch his hand lightly and invite him back to my hotel room for a drink. But it is neither, so I turn up the volume and talk instead about music, which I know nothing about.

What I Want

Sometimes I think I wish for: a slick, sleek ponytail to replace the unruly strands encircling my head.

I think I wish for: peep-toed pumps, a platinum band tucked neatly behind a perfect diamond ring.

I think maybe I want: the minivan, the Mercedes, Capri pants, contact lenses, a sparkling wooden smile.

But if I really wanted those things, wouldn't I brush my hair?

Reds

Karim taught me to drive stick shift on a dark road by "the lake"—a pit where water was deposited each monsoon when the city drowned.

The front windshield of his car was cracked from when he'd punched it and the windows were so tinted, I never could tell how late it was when we were driving around, smoking Marlboro Reds.

When we met, he was smoking Lights and I said he may as well smoke tampons. So he switched and we kept on. Me driving, then him.

Soap Opera

The children appear bathed and fed. I pose with them, place the picture in a frame, post it online and then send them to exit stage left. When they have satisfied their small roles, I defeat, battle and calculate. Allow the real drama to continue without them, under the soft light of people to whom I owe little. I play leading roles only, clip-on earrings to be pulled from my earlobes with a satisfying snap while I purr into the phone or narrow my eyes and fire daggers from my mouth at someone I will end up in bed with. I go on dates with lawyers and opera singers and other men who make me glad there are more men.

Glad that my bed is empty when I return home to my dark apartment, slip off my shoes, crawl under the covers.

Games

After all these cups, you ask how I take my coffee. I can never tell which part of the game you are playing.

Perfect Relationship

I imagine his hands on: her neck,
her hips. His breath in her ear, whispering
Tell me what you like. He knows what I like.

To be in a relationship with yourself,
you need to be able to sleep
on both sides of the bed.
You need to be the one
who remembers to pay the bills
and the one who knows to get up and dance
because you love this song.

I imagine him smiling that smile,
telling her how smart she is

You need to listen to the sound
of your own voice

telling her how wrong I am,
how he doesn't love me,
I am a wrecking ball.

You need to be the woman who
cries herself to sleep
because this world is so cold.

And the woman who wakes in armor
because she's going to change it.

> *Will he start to do things her way;*
> *will her womb swell with his child,*
> *will she be a better mother than I am?*

And those kids?
Love them as if they were your own—
but know that they are not yours,
you are borrowing them from themselves.
And when you have done for them
have put them to bed
you need to take yourself to bed
stroke your own hair
tell yourself that it's going to be okay
because you're going to make it okay

> *He could expose the secret truths:*
> *that I am weak,*
> *stupid, scared, dependent.*
> *That I am heartless, crazy.*
> *Unfaithful.*

You need to be faithful to yourself—
let your eyes, your hands, your mouth wander—
but know who you're coming home to.
To be in a relationship with yourself
you have to appreciate the rise of your own hip
under the covers and the line
of your own collarbone.
You need to look in the mirror and say
                              damn, girl.
And once in a while,

you'll need to look yourself in the eye and say,
you could've done better.
Demand of yourself what you know
you are capable of
forgive yourself when you make mistakes.
Lend yourself a hand when you fall

Can I imagine that he
will never
lift his hand to strike her head?
Will never curl his lip
and call her a whore?

When the world tells you
to lower your gaze
lift your face to the sun
raise your glass and your voice
let them know that you
will protect this woman
won't let her go
won't call her a lost cause
won't join them
when they turn on her

because no one will ever
love you this much
again.

In a Parallel Universe

None of this has happened.

You are there to break out in laughter with me in the freezer aisle in the grocery store. You are there when my car won't start and you are in the kitchen on taco night managing to bump your head on things and still somehow be graceful.

In a parallel universe, I am with you when I get the news—good or bad—I am with you when I feel like my skin and bones are not enough of a container to hold me. I turn to you when I want to cry in someone's arms.

Flying

Once my life was like airline travel; I stood in the correct lines, took off my shoes, put my laptop in the plastic bin, waited to board the plane according to the zone listed on my ticket. I smiled apologies when I misunderstood direction, and I quickly regrouped. I knew where I was going, I paid the fare, and I followed the rules to get there unhurried, I stood on the right side of the moving walkway. Others rushed by.

In this, my thirtieth year, I cleared my car of snow, filled my tires with air, paid bills online—for the first time. I earned a paycheck, wrote a research proposal, drove long distances in solitude to unfamiliar places. I have stayed in hotels by myself. I feel like an independent woman in a movie: sunglasses poised on my head, wearing a sheath dress and taking no shit. I'm accelerating forward, my cell phone rings, emails come in. When I stop moving and appreciate that this role will not end—this is who I really must be in order to maintain my world, I am crushed by fear.

Preparation

after Truth Thomas

I am waiting for rain to break the stillness
generations of gold bangles nose pin braided hair
let loose
steel in the eye veiled by
apparent surrender

I come from women whose men submit
women who give credit away
frown upon vanity—never look like you're trying

Women who can't help:
        comparing complexions
        turning hysterical
        apologizing when they've done no wrong

The first to jump without a landing
        the last to admit the compliment
when my mother says my daughters are like men

I am trying to unlearn that these hands were meant
to be decorated in henna and then put to work
I am Erica Cane self-portraits on the wall
Carly Quartermaine entitlement
Animaniacs, She-ra, Gem--
I am a hologram

I am generations of women giving orders from behind curtains
  working my way through the list of "good girls don't…"
    poems on the backs of my hands, tattoos where my
      mother won't see

I've been kneading bread, sewing diapers, absorbing blows
  I've worn fingerprints under my sleeves that don't match
    the smile on my face

I am waiting to grow the skin of the woman I will become.

The woman no one prepared me to be.

Purge

He comes over once in a while with dinner, always spends the night. Occasionally I bring a bottle of wine to his place and spend the night there. Unless I am very bored or very lonely, I don't wonder about him. To the best of my knowledge, he does not wonder about me. It has been a few weeks and I go to see him, late on a Friday, after a day of work and a poetry reading.

The premise of the movie *The Purge* is free license for a night: anyone can kill without consequence. Masked gunmen jump with automatic weapons from the backs of trucks and mow down strangers. There is no time to mourn. Bodies are abandoned, everyone moves on. There is a sequel to this movie. It is playing on the enormous television mounted on the wall when I enter.

He pours me a drink and leads me to the oversized sectional couch that fills his living room. He covers us both with a comforter. We make some conversation about mutual friends and current events, he snuggles next to me. Sex is why I am here, watching this ridiculous movie in this ridiculous bachelor pad. I go to the bathroom and take off my tights. I sit back next to him in my dress and bare legs. He takes my hand in both of his, places all three of our hands on my leg. *Now we're getting somewhere*, I think. He removes his hands and leaves mine on my leg.

On the screen, a family has holed up in their home, parents and adult children and their spouses turning this dark night into a sort of celebration. One daughter opens fire on the other after dinner. On this night, you take what you want.

I look at him, look at my watch. "I'm going to go." I kiss his cheek and get up. He walks me to the door. Hugs me. "Text me when you get home."

It is a forty-minute drive from his house to mine. After I brush my teeth, leave my clothes on the bathroom floor, and get into my bed, I think, *I should have been here two hours ago.*

I have spent nearly half of my very limited free time and energy trying to get laid. Struggling through stilted dinner conversation and responding to inane text messages over the course of several weeks to get to three dates, which I have determined is the decent number before sex. Then feeling like I should make it work because I put in all that effort.

He texts me two weeks later. He wants me to come over. He wants to come over. I would rather sleep with my books laid out on the bed beside me.

Degrees

I have been so drunk that I fell off a toilet seat and bruised my cheek.

I've been to meetings still smelling like whiskey from the night before.

I've taken tequila shots in an above ground pool with people I barely know.

I've snuck out of hotel rooms while the mistake was still sleeping.

I have said *I love you* and not meant it.

I have said *I love you* and pretended not to mean it.

I have said *I love you* and denied it later.

I do less of that now.

Grade me on a curve.

Known

Sometimes men bring me dinner. Or giant bottles of vodka already half empty. One or two may have brought me muscle relaxants wrapped in cellophane. When they point out my considerable flaws, I point out that I have never, will never, *could not possibly* move the door. *You're welcome to leave*, I tell them. I become too attached before I know them. Detach as soon as I know enough. They never meet my children.

But the people who share my life arrive hungry and thirsty, bearing rocks or shark teeth they've collected or art or ice cream or beer and flowers. They send handwritten letters that shine among the bills in my mailbox and I paper my walls with their words of affirmation. They embrace me when they arrive and again when they leave and while they are with me I don't think about how I look.

They—poets artists musicians accountants veterans gamblers teachers retirees bartenders alcoholics social workers ex-cons farmers comedians activists—come from far, remove their shoes and stretch out to fill my apartment, spilling onto the balcony to sit on the old futon covered in quilts and drink tea and smoke cigarettes after the kids have gone to bed. We tell stories and laugh about horrible things we know to be true. We have loud opinions that we negate over the course of our conversations. We argue. We eat and eat and eat. Drink less than we used to.

They sleep on the couch, or in the kids' beds when they are empty, on the balcony or in the wide space to the left on my king-sized bed. Wherever they sleep, I bring them coffee in the early morning when our faces are soft and vulnerable, our voices creaking. If the kids are home, Zaki stumbles in, snuggles into me. They witness our tenderness, and the sharp edge in my raised voice when I catch my children in a lie, or when I am harried and irritated about other things.

They are my friends from work, from high school and grad school and middle school and college and childhood and writing. Many of them don't know one another except in the stories I carry like bits of bread between them. Sometimes their schedules overlap, and my fairy godfriends are in my apartment together and it's like my birthday or my funeral. Everyone knows everything; I do not worry that a secret will come out. I have laid out all the splintered bits of me. I am known. Loved anyway.

Notes
On Truth-Telling

My sons have heard much of my writing. They hear me consider lines of poems aloud while I'm editing, they listen to the stories I've written about them. Because my time with them is limited, everything I do outside of our family is a sacrifice my children are making, and I make a concerted effort to involve them in the moments of celebration, rare as they are. Occasionally my older son, Sam, accompanies me to open mics and attends readings when I have the good fortune of landing them. Much of my writing deals with my dysfunctional relationship with their father, with whom I share custody. After one reading, my cousin's wife voiced concerns about Sam being exposed to these stories.

"How will he feel?" She asked. "He loves his father; he might feel destined to repeat those mistakes if he knows about them."

Parenting—life in general—is a high-stakes experiment. I don't know what the correct answer is. I can only do the best I can do today. I can only try to be better tomorrow. If Sam does feel destined or inclined to use his masculinity in the way his father does, I hope hearing my work will help him understand that the mistreatment of others has consequences. I hope that being caught between two people who have hurt one another so deeply, but are continually trying their best, can teach him to accept the gray in the world.

I hope it teaches him both how to apologize and how to forgive.

My children have not had an ordinary childhood. They do not have an ordinary mother—whatever that means. I am a writer, with all the eccentricities that seem to follow. I run writing and art workshops with veterans suffering from post-traumatic stress and mental illness. I come home from that work soggy, spent, a teabag steeped in trauma. Nothing in the world makes sense to me, so I am always wondering, often aloud. If I tried to shield them from this, I would be a cardboard cut-out of myself. They wouldn't know me, wouldn't know why I am who I am. The things I hear at work and have experienced during the course of my life would still appear in my shortcomings, would undoubtedly affect my relationships with the boys. They would stand as a barrier between us instead of serving as an opportunity for me to reveal myself, and for us to grow as individuals and in our bond as a family.

Of the many things I want for my children and myself, my chief desire is for us to be close. I want us to know one another and for our home to be a place where vulnerability is safe and questions are applauded. When my teenager admits his fears, I am proud of the strength he exhibits by doing so. When my seven-year-old was held after school because the things his too-strict, minutiae-driven teacher wants him to do in the classroom are "her goals, not mine," I was filled with admiration for his boldness and critical thinking (I was also mortified). My responsibility to these boys is not simply to insulate them from bodily harm and make sure they have the education and resources to carry the middle class torch that has been passed to them. I must prepare them to withstand life, and all the things I cannot protect them from. By showing an example of dishonesty (for dishonesty can exist in the silences we hold), by trying to appear invulnerable, I would teach my children that imperfection—*feeling*—is shameful. That grief and pain are burdens to struggle with in stoic solitude. In the muddy swamp of our emotional minds, guilt and shame flourish and choke us. In order to survive their lives, have meaningful relationships, and grow from their experiences, they must learn to recognize their emotions. They must feel empowered to give voice to their own perspectives, to consciously acknowledge the ways in which their journeys have shaped them. I have made and continue to make many mistakes—but I can think of no way to help them learn to honestly stumble forward other than by example.

In working with trauma survivors, the hardest person to help, aside from the one who absolutely refuses help, is the person who arrives with his arms out, palms up and says, "Fix it. Fix me." We as a society—as artists, teachers, pharmacists, psychiatrists, psychologists and social workers—cannot. We can offer wisdom and provide safe environments for self-reflection. We can help to identify the right questions, but we cannot answer them—and we cannot change the fact that neither the questions nor the answers will remain static. I often point out in writing groups within psychiatric treatment programs that "the trauma that brought you here will not be the last one you face. Life will keep hitting you."

Each of us can only truly know one particular life—our own. The task of knowing that life—its intricacies, its complex patterns of beauty and suffering and the ripples those experiences make upon our consciousnesses—is relentless. We must each learn to recognize the particular pitch of the voice within our head that doggedly chips away at our sense of self-worth, we must each learn what it feels like just before we lose control of our tempers, and we must find our own solutions, plot our own escape routes so that our bodies can continue to survive our minds. And as our lives continue to change and change us, we must keep abreast of who we are becoming. We must pivot, recalibrate, iron out new wrinkles, repair new wounds. Learning to ask questions is the closest any of us can come to knowing.

However, as certainly as our paths are individual, and lasting lessons cannot be impressed upon us, we require community. In *All About Love*, bell hooks quotes M. Scott Peck on the importance of finding and maintaining spaces where we can be ourselves, "'In and through community lies the salvation of the world.' Peck defines community as the coming together of a group of individuals 'who have learned how to communicate honestly with each other, whose relationships go deeper than their masks of composure . . .'" We seek out acceptance, but when an artificial construct of ourselves is what we present to the world, and that is what is accepted, we are miserable. The untold difficult stories of our own lives give weight to the nagging voice inside each of us, particularly in survivors of abuse, that says, *If people really knew you, they would reject you.* We are terrified of being exposed. So our instinct is often to keep people from knowing us, and the voice just gets louder. But honesty, though terrifying at the onset, neutralizes much of the self-doubt.

The collective experience of life is made up of a multitude of individual truths. Where these truths overlap they create deep pools of clarity. In facilitating writing workshops with people from vastly different backgrounds, I have learned there are emotional threads that are common across lives. Though the particulars and how they manifest are different, in the places where the truth of another experience, well told, touches a familiar chord, our own knowing is awakened and validated. In *Bird by Bird: Some Instructions on Writing and Life*, Anne Lamott says, "When writers make us shake our heads with the exactness of their prose and their truths, and even make us laugh about ourselves or life, our buoyancy is restored. We are given a shot at dancing with, or at least clapping along with, the absurdity of life, instead of being squashed by it over and over again." By sharing our individual truths and listening to the truths of others, we can clear the fog that separates what we have experienced from what we are *supposed* to have experienced.

Silence is dangerous. Truth telling is empowering, a necessary act of rebellion against the notion that our individual perspectives are somehow invalid. Secret keeping is central to the creation and maintenance of systems of abuse. When we abide by enforced silences we perpetuate these systems. By peering into the distorted mirrors that are held up all around us and pretending to recognize ourselves in the reflections, we encourage others to do the same. And when we observe others doing the same, we are flung further into our spirals of isolation. If the grief and hurt and trauma in each suffering person were boiled down, I believe what would remain is one question—"I have been through this, I have done this, I have seen this, I have regrets. Am I good enough?" Our job as a community of human beings is to answer the question with a resounding

"Yes."

Giving voice to our particular feelings and experiences, whether or not they align with the accepted narrative of a culture, community, movement, or relationship is never the easy route to take—our voices shake; there is an inherent vulnerability in self-exposure. But the consequences of silence are greater, for us as individuals, and for society as a whole. There are risks we take when we tell these stories. There is the fact that by the time the story travels from my life through my memory into your hands, dear reader, it will not quite be non-fiction. I invited you to walk with me through it but I did not always hold your hand. Sometimes I needed you to hold mine. Parts of this book were so difficult to write, I nearly gave up. Even now, as my fingers tap against the keyboard, I am nervous, looking for something else to do. *Have I put the milk carton back into the refrigerator? Shouldn't I be doing laundry?*

But here we are. We traveled this story together.

Thank you.

Works Consulted

Ackerman, Diane: *A Natural History of Love*. (Vintage, 1995)

Addonizio, Kim: *What Is This Thing Called Love: Poems*. (WW Norton & Company, 2005)

Bechdel, Alison: *Are You My Mother?* (Mariner Books, 2013)

Dillard, Annie: *The Writing Life*. (Harper Collins, 1990)

Gilligan, Carol: *The Birth of Pleasure*. (Vintage, 2003)

Hooks, Bell: *All About Love: New Visions*. (Harper Collins, 2001)

Lamott, Anne: *Bird by Bird: Some Instructions on Writing and Life*. (Anchor Books, 1995)

McGehee, J. Pittman: *The Paradox of Love*. (Bright Sky Press, 2011)

Rich, Adrienne Cecile: *Of Woman Born: Motherhood as Experience and Institution*. (WW Norton & Company, 1995)

Ryan, Christopher, and Cacilda Jethá: *Sex at Dawn: How We Mate, Why We Stray, and What It Means for Modern Relationships*. (Harper Collins, 2011)

Sendak, Maurice: *Where the Wild Things Are*. (Harper Collins, 1991)

Solnit, Rebecca: *The Faraway Nearby*. (Penguin Books, 2014)

In Gratitude

To my fairy godparents (has ever a person been so lucky as to have three?): Jocelyn Cullity, Walter Butts and Caryn Mirriam-Goldberg. For reading draft after draft as if they were laying eyes on it for the first time. For growing from mentors into friends and for helping me turn jagged truth into art.

To Kate Gale at Red Hen Press. Who believed, who believed, who believed. And edited (and edited and edited).

To Goddard College, an extraordinary, constantly evolving institution, committed to honoring the human capacity for growth and evolution. Not since my Montessori childhood have I felt so capable, so academically at home.

To the veterans, active duty service members, wounded, ill and injured warriors and all the people who care for them that I have had the great honor of knowing and working with. You have shown me new edges of the human experience, and have restored in me a faith in the human capacity for healing and perseverance.

To my beautiful sisters, Mona and Hooma Reza, my kick-ass brother-in-law Raj Din, and incredible cousins and family the world over. You didn't let me take myself too seriously or get too big for my boots. You held me while I cried.

To my dear Inshira and Jenna: narcissistically, I think of past selves when I am with you. Your unwavering love and admiration has brought me relief, perseverance and joy. To my nieces and nephews: Would my world be as bright without you in it? I am certain it would not.

To my friends, local and not: you have saved my life. You have reminded me to laugh, to get my nose out of books and dance, to stop being such a damn baby. For every late night conversation that ended abruptly with me needing to run and write because you shed light on something that had been shrouded in darkness. You know who you are. If you have to wonder if I mean you, then I probably don't.

To my mother, who is okay with imperfection, and in that is perfect. You have taught me how to love, how to make space at my table, how to laugh before the tears have dried.

And to my sons, my greatest teachers. May you learn half as much from me as I have from you. Your flashes of wisdom, your strength in the face of life's changes, your thoughtful questions, your kindness towards me, and your astonishing capacity for forgiveness have kept me afloat all these years, and my love for you has kept me from being swept away by grief.

Biographical Note

Seema Reza is a poet and essayist based outside of Washington, DC, where she coordinates and facilitates a unique hospital arts program that encourages the use of the arts as a tool for narration, self-care and socialization among a military population struggling with emotional and physical injuries. An alumnus of VONA and Goddard College, she was awarded the 2015 Col John Gioia Patriot Award by USO of Metropolitan Washington-Baltimore for her work with service members. *When the World Breaks Open* is her first book.